Good Housekeeping FAVORITE RECIPES

Easy Skillet Meals

Weeknight Country Captain

Good Housekeeping FAVORITE RECIPES

Easy Skillet Meals

Delicious One-Dish Cooking

HEARST BOOKS

A DIVISION OF STERLING PUBLISHING CO., INC.

NEW YORK

Copyright © 2005
by Hearst Communications, Inc.

Ellen Levine	**Editor in Chief**
Susan Westmoreland	**Food Director**
Susan Deborah Goldsmith	**Associate Food Director**
Delia Hammock	**Nutrition Director**
Sharon Franke	**Food Appliances Director**
Richard Eisenberg	**Special Projects Director**
Marilu Lopez	**Design Director**

Library of Congress
Cataloging-in-Publication Data

Good housekeeping easy skillet meals : simple to
make, easy to clean up, and very delicious / the
editors of Good housekeeping.
p. cm.
Includes index.
ISBN 1-58816-207-9
1. Skillet cookery. I. Title: Easy skillet meals.
II. Good housekeeping.
TX840.S55G66 2005
641.7'7--dc22

2004025001

10 9 8 7 6 5 4 3 2 1

Published by Hearst Books
A Division of Sterling Publishing Co., Inc.
387 Park Avenue South, New York, NY 10016

For information about custom editions,
special sales, premium and corporate purchases,
please contact Sterling Special Sales Department
at 800-805-5489 or
specialsales@sterlingpub.com.

Distributed in Canada by Sterling Publishing
c/o Canadian Manda Group, 165 Dufferin Street
Toronto, Ontario, Canada M6K 3H6

Distributed in Australia by Capricorn Link
(Australia) Pty. Ltd.
P.O. Box 704, Windsor, NSW 2756 Australia

Manufactured in China

ISBN 1-58816-207-9

CONTENTS

Three-Cheese Polenta Pizza

FOREWORD

Skillet meals are so easy to make and so good, you'll probably find yourself making them often. In that case, you may want to know what kind of skillet is best. I do most of my cooking (from making buttermilk pancakes to stir-frying broccoli) in a skillet, so I rely on more than one. Friends are surprised when they come for dinner and don't find shiny matching pots and pans, but my philosophy is to use what works best for each task.

My black 12-inch cast-iron skillet is a must for searing burgers, steak, and herb-rubbed pork chops, even oven-roasting a whole chicken. My cousin Judith gave me the pan in 1975 as a piece of Americana right after I finished French cooking school. This old reliable is also my standby for frittatas—my grandmother and my mom both used a cast-iron pan to make them, so I feel like I'm carrying on the tradition. (After using, I wash the pan with soapy water the way my mother always does, then I dry it over a medium gas flame—waiting, like my mom does, to hear the last drop of water sizzle—and lightly rub the interior with vegetable oil on a paper towel.)

For nonstick needs, I reach for a rather expensive, brand-name 12-inch pan. It was a major investment, but it's worth it to me because it has multiple layers of high-quality nonstick coating to make it extra durable. I love having a lot of surface area for cooking and not needing to use much fat (just a teaspoon or so of olive oil).

The third skillet in my arsenal is a medium-priced nonstick stainless-steel pan that my husband, Rip, bought for me. It's 8 inches across the top and a mere 6 inches on the bottom, with beautiful sloping sides, perfect for making the kind of open-face omelet our 10-year-old son, Lucio, loves so much. When he was younger he sat on the counter anticipating the moment I would turn out the omelet so he could grate Parmesan all over the top, happiness written on his face. Now he is by my side at the stove. Is it any wonder I love my humble skillet?

Susan Westmoreland
FOOD DIRECTOR, *Good Housekeeping*

SKILLET SIMPLE

On a busy weeknight, nothing beats a skillet meal. You can cook a complete supper in a few minutes, then put it on the table in the same skillet in which it was cooked. The infinite variety of skillet recipes—this book has over 115—means that you can serve a different supper each night—only the fool-proof preparation method stays the same.

Although skillet meals are perfect for today's busy cooks, there is nothing new about cooking supper in one pan over a single heat source. In fact, it's an American tradition. In Colonial America, women prepared skillet meals in their open fireplaces; in the nineteenth-century, cowboys stirred up spicy mixtures in skillets set over their campfires, and twentieth-century immigrants were sustained by skillet recipes brought from Europe, Africa, and Asia. During the mid-twentieth century fancy skillet meals were often flamed tableside at upscale restaurants.

You'll find delicious recipes from all of these traditions in the pages that follow. So you're sure to find a tantalizing option for every occasion. The kids want comfort food? No problem. Company dropping in and you need something impressive, fast? You can do it. Looking for something exotic. It's right here. Simply select your recipe and head for the stove.

GETTING STARTED

Skillet meals require no special equipment; you probably have everything you need in your kitchen right now—a skillet with a lid, a knife, vegetable peeler, cutting board, and spatula. While we encourage you to start cooking with whatever equipment you have on hand, there are some things to keep in mind as you decide which pan to use or before you purchase any new stovetop cookware.

Skillet Smarts

• **Size matters.** If the recipe suggests using a certain size skillet, there is probably a good reason. Either you need that amount of surface to adequately brown the foods that go in first, or you need the total volume of the pan to hold all the foods you will be adding later.

• **Heavy helps.** Make sure you select a heavy skillet so that the heat is distributed evenly. A stainless-steel skillet with an aluminum core or an enameled cast-iron skillet is a good choice. Avoid light-weight skillets and those with thin sides even if they have a heavy bottom. Foods can burn easily when they touch the overheated metal on the sides.

• **Put a lid on it.** Although you won't use them all the time, lids are important for skillet recipes where you want to steam or braise the food. So make sure you have a sturdy lid to fit each of your skillets securely.

• **Cast iron care.** If you have inherited a well-seasoned cast-iron skillet, treasure it. This kitchen classic will cook evenly and look good on the table. Always wash a cast iron skillet by hand and dry it thoroughly after each cleaning, and it will serve you well. Periodically reseason by rubbing it with vegetable shortening and heating it in a low oven.

Skillet Substitutes

• **Chicken fryer.** Skillet meals can also be cooked in a chicken fryer, which is a heavy skillet that has 3- or 4-inch high sides, and is usually wide and deep enough for a meal to serve six. They often come with a heavy domed lid that is handy when cooking with moist heat.

• **Wok.** A good choice for many skillet meals, a wok is particularly useful for cooking thinly-sliced meats and vegetables. The food can first be seared on the bottom and then moved up the sides of the wok. Here it can finish cooking slowly and stay warm while the remaining ingredients are cooked in the bottom of the pan. For best results, use a wok with a heavy bottom cooking surface and a sturdy ring so that it sits evenly over the heat source.

Before You Buy

• **Looks count.** If you are purchasing a new skillet, choose one that is attractive enough to serve from. If you prepare your meal in a skillet that can be taken to the table, the food will stay warm longer because of the residual heat. Also, you won't have to transfer foods to a serving dish, which will make clean-up easier.

• **The right finish.** A non-stick finish is not necessary for most skillet meals. However, if you are considering purchasing a skillet with a non-stick finish, be sure to read the current literature on the safety of the various finishes. If you have a non-stick skillet, make sure it is never heated without something in it, and never use it over high heat.

STOVE-TOP STRATEGIES

Skillet meals are some of the easiest to prepare because the technique is so logical. No matter which recipe you choose, the sequence of steps is about the same. Ingredients are assembled and prepared for cooking then added to the skillet in order—from those that take the longest to cook to those that cook most quickly. The food is cooked either in oil, butter, or shortening in a skillet without a lid or with a liquid in a covered skillet. Sometimes the juices are thickened to make a sauce.

Although the process seems quite straight-forward, we discovered, as we tested a wide variety of skillet meals in the Good Housekeeping kitchens, a number of ways to ensure a perfect meal each time and to make the job even easier. Here's what we recommend:

• **The measure of success.** Even though the recipes are simple, it is important to use standard measuring equipment. Don't be tempted to use tableware for measuring; use standard dry measuring cups for dry ingredients, glass measuring cups for liquids, and standard measuring spoons when measuring tablespoons and teaspoons.

• **Ready for action.** In addition to the perfect pan, be sure to get out tongs and potholders before starting your meal. That way they'll be ready to use the moment you need them. Tongs are better for stir-frying than metal spatulas because they don't break the vegetables and are excellent for turning one piece of meat at a time. There are some with heatproof silicone tips that won't scratch your nonstick pans.

• **Prepare ahead.** Because skillet meals cook quickly, it's a good idea to assemble and rinse, peel, slice, or chop all the ingredients before you start

Curried Sweet Potatoes & Lentils

to cook. That way nothing will overcook while you are preparing the next ingredient.

• **Timing is everything.** Don't forget to set out a kitchen timer. Skillet meals can be done before you know it, so it's wise to have a timer remind you it's time to pull the skillet off the stove.

• **Prevent sticking.** Unless the recipe directs otherwise, preheat the oil or butter in the skillet before adding any other ingredients. Food added to a cold pan is more likely to stick.

• **Oil substitutions.** If a recipe calls for a specific oil for sautéing or stir-frying, you can substitute another oil without affecting the recipe. However, it is not a good idea to substitute butter or shortening unless you reduce the cooking temperature, as solid fats have a lower smoking point than oils and might burn.

• **Replacing fresh herbs.** If the directions call for 1 tablespoon of a fresh herb, and you don't have it you can substitute 1 teaspoon dried. Be sure to crumble dried herbs in the palms of your hands before adding to your food to release more of their flavor.

• **Check dried herbs.** Even the finest quality dried herbs begin to lose flavor as soon as the jar is opened and should be used or replaced within 6 months of opening. Before cooking, be sure your dried herbs are fresh.

• **Lid theory.** If a skillet meal is supposed to be prepared without a lid, please don't use one. The lid allows moisture to collect in the pan, which means it will also reduce browning, soften the crumbs used for breading, and toughen tender cuts of meat. Lids are best when you want the food to steam as it cooks and to tenderize the vegetables quickly. The recipes in this book will specify when and how to use a lid.

• **Splatter not.** A wire mesh splatter guard is a big help when sautéing or frying moist foods and a lid is not called for. The guard will catch the oil or fat and keep it from splashing onto countertops and clothing. At the same time a splatter guard releases steam rather than trapping it, so the food does not overcook or become mushy.

POULTRY

Thai Chicken with Basil
recipe on page 50

Chicken Cacciatore

Food prepared *alla cacciatore*, "hunter style," includes mushrooms in the sauce. This is the kind of home cooking that found its way first into Italian restaurants and then into American kitchens. Serve over wide noodles (such as pappardelle or fettuccine).

PREP: 15 MINUTES   COOK: 40 MINUTES
MAKES 4 MAIN-DISH SERVINGS.

2 tablespoons olive oil
1 chicken (3$^{1}/_{2}$ pounds), cut into
   8 pieces and skin removed from
   all but wings
3 tablespoons all-purpose flour
1 medium onion, finely chopped
4 garlic cloves, crushed with
   garlic press

8 ounces mushrooms, trimmed and
   thickly sliced
1 can (14 to 16 ounces) tomatoes
$^{1}/_{2}$ teaspoon salt
$^{1}/_{2}$ teaspoon dried oregano, crumbled
$^{1}/_{4}$ teaspoon dried sage
$^{1}/_{8}$ teaspoon ground red pepper
   (cayenne)

1. In nonstick 12-inch skillet, heat oil over medium–high heat until very hot. On waxed paper, coat chicken with flour, shaking off excess. Add chicken to skillet, and cook until golden brown, about 5 minutes per side. With slotted spoon, transfer chicken pieces to bowl as they are browned.
2. Add onion and garlic to skillet. Reduce heat to medium–low and cook, stirring occasionally, until onion is tender, about 5 minutes. Add mushrooms and cook, stirring frequently, until just tender, about 3 minutes.
3. Add tomatoes with their juice, breaking them up with side of spoon. Add salt, oregano, sage, ground red pepper, and chicken, and heat to boiling over high heat. Reduce heat; cover and simmer until juices run clear when thickest part of chicken is pierced with tip of knife, about 25 minutes.
4. Transfer chicken to serving bowl. Spoon sauce over chicken.

Each serving: About 371 calories, 44g protein, 18g carbohydrate, 13g total fat (3g saturated), 133mg cholesterol, 608mg sodium.

Chicken Mole

A thick, rich, dark brown Mexican sauce, mole (MO-lay) is traditionally made with dried chiles, spices, seeds such as pumpkin, nuts, and a small amount of unsweetened chocolate. Here's our version, which should be served over rice or crisp tortillas to soak up the spicy mole.

PREP: 10 MINUTES   COOK: 45 MINUTES
MAKES 6 MAIN-DISH SERVINGS.

1 can (14 1/2 ounces) diced tomatoes
1 can (4 to 4 1/2 ounces) chopped
  mild green chiles
1/2 cup whole blanched almonds
1/2 small onion, coarsely chopped
1 small garlic clove, peeled
1 tablespoon chili powder
1 teaspoon ground cumin
1 teaspoon ground coriander
3/4 teaspoon ground cinnamon
3/4 teaspoon salt
1/2 teaspoon sugar
1 tablespoon olive oil
3 pounds bone-in chicken parts, skin
  removed from all but wings
1/2 square (1/2 ounce) unsweetened
  chocolate, chopped
1/4 cup water
2 tablespoons chopped fresh cilantro

1. Prepare mole sauce: In blender or in food processor with knife blade attached, puree tomatoes, chiles, almonds, onion, garlic, chili powder, cumin, coriander, cinnamon, salt, and sugar until smooth.

2. In nonstick 12-inch skillet, heat oil over medium-high heat until very hot. Add chicken and cook until golden brown, about 5 minutes per side; transfer chicken pieces to large bowl as they are browned.

3. Add mole sauce, chocolate, and water to skillet; cook, stirring, until chocolate melts. Return chicken to skillet; heat to boiling. Reduce heat; cover and simmer until chicken juices run clear when thickest part of thigh is pierced with tip of knife, 30 to 35 minutes. To serve, sprinkle with chopped cilantro.

Each serving: About 263 calories, 27g protein, 9g carbohydrate, 14g total fat (3g saturated), 76mg cholesterol, 617mg sodium.

Skillet-Braised Chicken

The secret to this full-bodied dish is cooking the chicken in two steps. First sear it in hot oil to seal in juices and create a rich, browned flavor. Then simmer it, covered, in liquid until tender and cooked through. Pair with vegetable purees, polenta, or risotto to soak up all the savory sauce.

PREP: 20 MINUTES   COOK: 45 MINUTES
MAKES 4 MAIN-DISH SERVINGS.

2 tablespoons vegetable oil
8 bone-in chicken thighs (about
   2¹/₂ pounds), skin and fat removed
1 teaspoon salt
1 large onion (12 ounces),
   coarsely chopped
4 medium carrots, peeled and
   chopped

1 large stalk celery, chopped
1 can (14¹/₂ to 16 ounces) Italian-
   style stewed tomatoes
chopped fresh parsley and grated
   lemon peel (optional)

1. In nonstick 12-inch skillet, heat oil over medium–high heat until hot. Add chicken thighs; sprinkle with salt. Cook chicken until golden on both sides, about 5 minutes per side. Transfer to bowl.

2. To drippings in skillet, add onion, carrots, and celery, and cook, stirring frequently, until vegetables are lightly browned, about 10 minutes.

3. Return chicken thighs to skillet. Stir in stewed tomatoes; heat to boiling over high heat. Reduce heat to low. Cover and simmer until juices run clear when thickest part of thigh is pierced with tip of knife, about 25 minutes. Serve sprinkled with chopped parsley and grated lemon peel, if you like.

Each serving: About 440 calories, 42g protein, 18g carbohydrate, 21g total fat (5g saturated), 190mg cholesterol, 935mg sodium.

Chicken and Sweet-Potato Stew

Coat chicken thighs with an exotic mix of cumin and cinnamon, then simmer with beta–carotene–rich sweet potatoes in a creamy peanut butter sauce. Delectable over brown rice.

PREP: 20 MINUTES   COOK: 45 MINUTES
MAKES 4 MAIN-DISH SERVINGS.

4 medium bone-in chicken thighs (about 1 1/2 pounds), skin and fat removed
1 teaspoon ground cumin
1/4 teaspoon ground cinnamon
1 tablespoon olive oil
3 medium sweet potatoes (about 1 1/2 pounds), peeled and cut into 1/2-inch chunks

1 medium onion, sliced
1 can (28 ounces) tomatoes in juice
3 tablespoons natural peanut butter
1/2 teaspoon salt
1/4 teaspoon crushed red pepper
2 garlic cloves, peeled
1/4 cup packed fresh cilantro leaves plus 2 tablespoons chopped cilantro leaves

1. Rub chicken thighs with cumin and cinnamon; set aside.
2. In nonstick 12-inch skillet, heat oil over medium heat. Add sweet potatoes and onion, and cook, stirring occasionally, until onion is tender, 12 to 15 minutes. Transfer sweet-potato mixture to plate.
3. Increase heat to medium-high. Add seasoned chicken, and cook until chicken is lightly browned on both sides, about 5 minutes.
4. Meanwhile, drain tomatoes, reserving juice. Coarsely chop tomatoes and set aside. In blender at high speed or in food processor with knife blade attached, blend tomato juice, peanut butter, salt, crushed red pepper, garlic, and 1/4 cup cilantro leaves until smooth.
5. Add sweet-potato mixture, peanut butter sauce, and chopped tomatoes to skillet with chicken; heat to boiling over high heat. Reduce heat to low; cover and simmer until juices run clear when thickest part of thigh is pierced with tip of knife, about 25 minutes. To serve, sprinkle with chopped cilantro.

Each serving: About 410 calories, 26g protein, 50g carbohydrate, 12g total fat (2g saturated), 76mg cholesterol, 725mg sodium.

Spicy Moroccan Stew

This dish is delicious all by itself, or served the way we like it best, with piping hot couscous.

PREP: 30 MINUTES   COOK: 40 MINUTES
MAKES 4 MAIN-DISH SERVINGS.

8 ounces peeled baby carrots (half 16-ounce bag)
2 tablespoons all-purpose flour
1 teaspoon ground cumin
1/2 teaspoon ground coriander
1/4 teaspoon ground red pepper (cayenne)
1/4 teaspoon coarsely ground black pepper
1/8 teaspoon ground cinnamon
3/4 teaspoon salt
1 tablespoon vegetable oil
8 medium bone-in chicken thighs (about 2 pounds bones), skin and fat removed

1 medium onion, sliced
2 medium zucchini (8 ounces each), each cut lengthwise in half, then crosswise into 1/4-inch-thick slices
1 can (28 ounces) tomatoes in puree
1 can (15 to 19 ounces) garbanzo beans, rinsed and drained
1 package (10 ounces) couscous (Moroccan pasta)
1 cup packed fresh cilantro leaves, chopped

1. In 10-inch skillet, heat *1 inch water* to boiling over high heat. Add carrots; heat to boiling. Reduce heat to low; cover and simmer until carrots are just tender–crisp, about 5 minutes. Drain carrots; set aside.

2. Meanwhile, in large ziptight plastic bag, combine flour, cumin, coriander, ground red pepper, black pepper, cinnamon, and 1/2 teaspoon salt. Add chicken and toss until evenly coated.

3. In nonstick 12-inch skillet, heat oil over medium-high heat until hot. Add chicken and cook until evenly browned, about 5 minutes per side. With tongs, transfer chicken to large bowl.

4. Reduce heat to medium. Add onion, zucchini, and remaining 1/4 teaspoon salt, and cook, stirring occasionally, until onion is lightly browned, 8 to 10 minutes. Add carrots and *1/4 cup water*, and cook 5 minutes longer.

5. To vegetables in skillet, add tomatoes with puree, garbanzo beans, and chicken; heat to boiling over medium-high heat, stirring and breaking up

tomatoes with side of spoon. Reduce heat to medium-low; cover and simmer until juices run clear when thickest part of thigh is pierced with knife, about 10 minutes.

6. Meanwhile, prepare couscous as label directs.

7. To serve, spoon couscous onto large platter; top with chicken mixture. Sprinkle with chopped cilantro.

Each serving: About 465 calories, 38g protein, 53g carbohydrate, 12g total fat (2g saturated), 110mg cholesterol, 1,540mg sodium.

Spicy Moroccan Stew

Mediterranean Sweet & Sour Chicken

We dressed up chicken thighs with sweet figs, salty olives, red wine vinegar, and a touch of brown sugar—a memorable flavor combination. If arugula is not available, substitute baby spinach or watercress.

PREP: 5 MINUTES   COOK: 20 MINUTES
MAKES 4 MAIN-DISH SERVINGS.

2 teaspoons olive oil
8 small bone-in chicken thighs (about 2 pounds)
1/4 teaspoon salt
2 garlic cloves, crushed with garlic press
1/2 cup chicken broth
1/4 cup red wine vinegar

2 teaspoons cornstarch
2 teaspoons brown sugar or to taste
3/4 cup (about half 10-ounce package) Mission figlets, each cut in half
1/4 cup chopped pimiento-stuffed olives (salad olives)
5 ounces baby arugula, trimmed

1. In nonstick 12-inch skillet, heat oil over medium-high heat until very hot. Add chicken and sprinkle with salt; cook until chicken is browned and juices run clear when thickest part of thigh is pierced with tip of knife, 8 to 10 minutes per side. Transfer chicken to plate. Add garlic to skillet, and cook, stirring, 30 seconds.

2. Meanwhile, in cup, with wire whisk, mix broth, vinegar, cornstarch, and sugar.

3. Stir broth mixture and add to skillet; heat to boiling. Boil, stirring until browned bits are loosened from bottom of skillet and sauce has thickened slightly, about 1 minute. Stir in figlets and olives; return chicken with any juices to skillet and heat through.

4. To serve, arrange arugula on 4 dinner plates. Spoon chicken mixture over arugula.

Each serving: About 375 calories, 38g protein, 30g carbohydrate, 11g total fat (2g saturated), 150mg cholesterol, 630mg sodium.

Asian Chicken Thighs

Sautéed boneless chicken thighs stay moist while broccoli flowerets turn tender-crisp in a robust soy, ginger, and brown-sugar pan sauce.

PREP: 10 MINUTES   COOK: 15 MINUTES
MAKES 4 MAIN-DISH SERVINGS.

1 1/4 pounds boneless chicken thighs, skin removed and each cut in half
1/4 teaspoon coarsely ground black pepper
3/4 cup water

3 tablespoons soy sauce
1 tablespoon grated, peeled fresh ginger
1 tablespoon brown sugar
1 bag (16 ounces) broccoli flowerets

1. Heat nonstick 12-inch skillet over medium heat until hot. Add the chicken thighs; sprinkle with pepper. Cook chicken until lightly browned, about 5 minutes per side.

2. Meanwhile, in measuring cup, with fork, mix water, soy sauce, ginger, and sugar until well blended.

3. Add soy sauce mixture and broccoli to skillet with chicken; heat to boiling. Cover and cook over medium-high heat, stirring occasionally, until broccoli is tender-crisp and juices run clear when thickest part of thigh is pierced with tip of knife, 5 to 7 minutes.

Each serving: About 220 calories, 32g protein, 11g carbohydrate, 6g total fat (2g saturated), 118mg cholesterol, 890mg sodium.

Southwest Chicken Stew

Southwest Chicken Stew

A flavor-packed combo of chicken thighs, potatoes, corn, and beans is simmered together, then thickened with crushed tortilla chips.

PREP: 25 MINUTES   COOK: 30 MINUTES
MAKES 6 MAIN-DISH SERVINGS.

1 teaspoon olive oil
6 large bone-in chicken thighs (about 2 pounds), skin and fat removed
1 medium onion, chopped
2 jalapeño chiles, seeded and minced
2 garlic cloves, crushed with garlic press
3/4 teaspoon ground cumin
1/2 teaspoon dried oregano
1 pound medium red potatoes, cut into 1 1/2-inch pieces

1 can (15 to 19 ounces) white kidney beans (cannellini), rinsed and drained
1 can (15 1/4 ounces) whole-kernel corn, drained
1 can (14 1/2 ounces) chicken broth
1 teaspoon salt
1/4 cup crushed baked tortilla chips
1/2 cup loosely packed fresh cilantro leaves, chopped

1. In deep nonstick 12-inch skillet, heat oil over medium-high heat until hot. Add chicken and cook until browned, 3 to 4 minutes per side. Transfer chicken to plate.

2. To same skillet, add onion, jalapeños, garlic, cumin, and oregano, and cook over medium heat, covered, until onion is golden, about 5 minutes, stirring occasionally.

3. Return chicken to skillet. Add potatoes, beans, corn, broth, and salt; heat to boiling. Reduce heat to medium-low and simmer, covered, until potatoes are fork-tender and juices run clear when thickest part of thigh is pierced with tip of knife, about 15 minutes, stirring occasionally.

4. Stir in tortilla chips, and cook, uncovered, until mixture thickens slightly, about 2 minutes. Add cilantro just before serving.

Each serving: About 365 calories, 31g protein, 44g carbohydrate, 7g total fat (2g saturated), 98mg cholesterol, 1,115mg sodium.

Bow Ties with Chicken & Wild Mushrooms

A delicious medley of shiitake, oyster, and white mushrooms, tossed with boneless chicken thighs, a splash of cream, and brandy.

PREP: 20 MINUTES   COOK: 25 MINUTES
MAKES 4 MAIN-DISH SERVINGS.

12 ounces bow-tie pasta
1 teaspoon olive oil
1 pound skinless, boneless chicken thighs, cut into 1-inch pieces
3/4 teaspoon salt
1/4 teaspoon coarsely ground black pepper
1 tablespoon butter or margarine
8 ounces white mushrooms, trimmed and thinly sliced
4 ounces oyster mushrooms, tough stems removed and caps thinly sliced

4 ounces shiitake mushrooms, stems removed and caps thinly sliced
1 medium onion, cut in half, then thinly sliced crosswise
1 garlic clove, crushed with garlic press
1 cup frozen peas
1/4 cup heavy or whipping cream
2 tablespoons brandy

1. In large saucepot, cook pasta as label directs.

2. Meanwhile, in nonstick 12-inch skillet, heat oil over medium-high heat until hot. Add chicken; sprinkle with 1/2 teaspoon salt and pepper, and cook just until chicken loses its pink color throughout, stirring frequently, about 5 minutes. Transfer chicken to plate; keep warm.

3. In same skillet, melt butter. Add mushrooms, onion, garlic, and the remaining 1/4 teaspoon salt, and cook, stirring frequently, until vegetables are tender and golden, about 15 minutes. Stir in frozen peas, cream, and brandy; heat to boiling. Remove skillet from heat.

4. When pasta is done, remove *1/2 cup pasta cooking water*. Drain pasta; return to saucepot. Add mushroom mixture, chicken, and reserved pasta cooking water; toss to combine.

Each serving: About 625 calories, 39g protein, 79g carbohydrate, 16g total fat (7g saturated), 122mg cholesterol, 711mg sodium.

Carolina Chicken Pilau

This simple recipe, made with bacon, onion, and chicken, is based on an old-fashioned Southern rice dish. For best flavor, cook the chicken breasts on the bone. If you have time, remove the chicken from the bone, shred the meat, and return it to the rice mixture; toss before serving.

PREP: 20 MINUTES   COOK: 45 MINUTES
MAKES 4 MAIN-DISH SERVINGS.

1 teaspoon olive oil
4 small bone-in chicken breast halves
  (about 2 3/4 pounds), skin removed
2 slices bacon, cut into
  1/4-inch pieces
1 large onion (12 ounces), cut
  lengthwise in half, then thinly
  sliced crosswise

1 cup regular long-grain white rice
1 can (14 1/2 ounces) chicken broth
1/4 teaspoon salt
1/4 teaspoon coarsely ground
  black pepper
1/2 cup water
1/2 cup loosely packed fresh parsley
  leaves, chopped

1. In nonstick 12-inch skillet, heat oil over medium-high heat until hot. Add chicken and cook until golden, about 4 minutes per side. Transfer chicken to plate. Reduce heat to medium; add bacon and cook, until browned, stirring frequently, about 4 minutes. With slotted spoon transfer bacon to paper towels to drain. Discard all but 2 teaspoons bacon drippings from skillet.

2. Add onion to skillet, and cook, covered, until tender and lightly browned, about 10 minutes, stirring occasionally. Add rice and stir until evenly coated. Stir in bacon, broth, salt, pepper, and water. Return chicken to skillet; heat to boiling over medium-high heat. Reduce heat to medium-low, and cook, covered, until juices run clear when thickest part of chicken is pierced with tip of knife and rice is tender, 20 to 25 minutes. Sprinkle with parsley to serve.

Each serving: About 390 calories, 36g protein, 41g carbohydrate, 8g total fat (2g saturated), 81mg cholesterol, 725mg sodium.

Skillet Chicken Potpie

This healthy version of the traditional favorite is made with skinless chicken breasts, a low-fat cream sauce, and a dumpling-like biscuit topping whipped up from an all-purpose baking mix.

PREP: 25 MINUTES   COOK: 40 MINUTES
MAKES 6 MAIN-DISH SERVINGS.

1 lemon
2 teaspoons olive oil
1 1/4 pounds skinless, boneless
 chicken breast halves (about 4
 medium), cut into 1-inch pieces
2 medium carrots, peeled and cut
 into 1/2-inch pieces
1 medium onion, finely chopped
1 medium stalk celery, thinly sliced
1 can (14 1/2 ounces) fat-free
 chicken broth

1/2 teaspoon salt
1/4 teaspoon dried thyme
1/8 teaspoon ground black pepper
3 tablespoons cornstarch
1 1/2 cups plus 1/3 cup nonfat (skim)
 milk
1 cup reduced-fat all-purpose
 baking mix
1 cup frozen peas

1. From lemon, with vegetable peeler, remove 3 strips peel (about 3" by 1" each); set aside.

2. In deep nonstick 12-inch skillet, heat 1 teaspoon oil over medium-high heat until hot. Add half of chicken, and cook until golden, 3 to 5 minutes, stirring occasionally. Transfer chicken to plate; repeat with remaining chicken. Set aside.

3. In same skillet, heat remaining 1 teaspoon oil; add carrots, onion, and celery, and cook over medium-high heat, stirring occasionally, 5 minutes. Add broth, salt, thyme, pepper, and lemon peel; heat to boiling. Reduce heat to low; cover and simmer the mixture until vegetables are tender, about 10 minutes.

4. Meanwhile, in medium bowl, with wire whisk, mix the cornstarch and 1 1/2 cups milk until smooth. In small bowl, stir baking mix with remaining 1/3 cup milk until blended; set dough aside.

5. Stir cornstarch mixture into vegetables in skillet; heat to boiling over medium-high heat. Boil, stirring, 1 minute. Add chicken and peas; heat to boiling. Remove lemon peel and discard.

6. Drop dough by tablespoons over chicken mixture. Reduce heat to medium-low; cover and simmer until biscuits are cooked through, about 10 minutes.

Each serving: About 270 calories, 28g protein, 28g carbohydrate, 5g total fat (1g saturated), 56mg cholesterol, 845mg sodium.

Skillet Chicken Potpie

Tarragon & Grape Chicken

Cloaked in a creamy pan sauce, these chicken breasts are elegant enough for company, easy enough for a weeknight supper. Quick cooking barley or a white-and-wild rice blend makes a nice accompaniment.

Prep: 15 minutes   Cook: 20 minutes
Makes 4 main-dish servings.

4 medium skinless, boneless chicken breast halves (about 1 1/4 pounds)
1/2 teaspoon salt
1/4 teaspoon coarsely ground black pepper
1 teaspoon olive oil
2 teaspoons butter or margarine
3 medium shallots, minced (about 1/3 cup)

1/4 cup dry white wine
1/4 cup chicken broth
1/4 cup half-and-half or light cream
1 cup seedless red and/or green grapes, each cut in half
1 tablespoon chopped fresh tarragon

1. Sprinkle chicken with 1/4 teaspoon salt and pepper.
2. In nonstick 12-inch skillet, heat oil over medium-high heat until hot. Add chicken and cook 6 minutes. Reduce heat to medium; turn chicken over, and cook until juices run clear when thickest part of breast is pierced with tip of knife, 6 to 8 minutes longer. Transfer the chicken to a platter; keep warm.
3. In same skillet, melt butter over medium-low heat. Add shallots and remaining 1/4 teaspoon salt, and cook, stirring, until tender and golden, 3 to 5 minutes. Stir in wine; cook 30 seconds. Stir in broth, half-and-half, grapes, and tarragon. Return chicken to skillet; heat through.

Each serving: About 255 calories, 34g protein, 10g carbohydrate, 8g total fat (5g saturated), 103mg cholesterol, 437mg sodium.

Tarragon & Grape Chicken

Greek-Style Chicken

Greek-Style Chicken

Kalamata olives and feta cheese add zip to this easy chicken supper.
Serve with hot crusty bread and a green salad

PREP: 15 MINUTES   COOK: 20 MINUTES
MAKES 4 MAIN-DISH SERVINGS.

4 medium skinless, boneless chicken
  breast halves (about 1 1/4 pounds)
1/4 teaspoon salt
1/4 teaspoon coarsely ground
  black pepper
3 teaspoons olive oil
1 small onion, finely chopped
4 medium plum tomatoes (about
  12 ounces), cut into 1/4-inch pieces

1/4 cup Kalamata olives, pitted
  and chopped
1 tablespoon fresh lemon juice
1/4 cup water
1/2 cup crumbled feta cheese
2 tablespoons chopped fresh parsley

1. Sprinkle chicken with salt and 1/8 teaspoon pepper.
2. In nonstick 12-inch skillet, heat 1 teaspoon oil over medium-high heat until hot. Add chicken and cook 6 minutes. Reduce heat to medium; turn chicken and cook until juices run clear when thickest part of breast is pierced with tip of knife, 6 to 8 minutes longer. Transfer chicken to a platter; keep warm.
3. In same skillet, heat remaining 2 teaspoons oil over medium-low heat. Add onion and cook, stirring, until tender and golden, about 5 minutes. Add tomatoes, olives, lemon juice, water, and remaining 1/8 teaspoon pepper and cook, stirring, until the tomatoes release their juice, about 1 minute. Stir in feta and parsley.
4. To serve, pour tomato mixture over chicken.

Each serving: About 275 calories, 36g protein, 8g carbohydrate, 11g total fat (3g saturated), 95mg cholesterol, 525mg sodium.

Chicken with Asparagus & Mushrooms

If fresh shiitakes are unavailable, use 1 ounce of dried reconstituted ones. Be sure to rinse and drain them before slicing.

PREP: 20 MINUTES   COOK: 25 MINUTES
MAKES 4 MAIN-DISH SERVINGS.

4 medium skinless, boneless chicken breast halves (about 1 1/4 pounds)
3/4 teaspoon salt
1/4 teaspoon coarsely ground black pepper
3 teaspoons olive oil
1 medium onion, chopped
4 ounces shiitake mushrooms, stems removed and caps thinly sliced

4 ounces white mushrooms, trimmed and thinly sliced
1 1/2 pounds asparagus, trimmed and cut into 2-inch pieces
1/4 cup water
1/2 cup half-and-half or light cream

1. Sprinkle chicken with 1/4 teaspoon salt and pepper.
2. In nonstick 12-inch skillet, heat 1 teaspoon olive oil over medium-high heat until hot. Add chicken and cook 6 minutes. Reduce heat to medium; turn chicken and cook, until juices run clear when thickest part of breast is pierced with tip of knife, 6 to 8 minutes longer. Transfer chicken to platter; keep warm.
3. In same skillet, heat remaining 2 teaspoons olive oil over medium heat until hot. Add onion and mushrooms and cook, stirring frequently, until vegetables are tender and liquid has evaporated, about 5 minutes.
4. Add asparagus, water, and remaining 1/2 teaspoon salt to mushroom mixture; heat to boiling. Cook, stirring often, until asparagus is tender-crisp, about 5 minutes. Stir in half-and-half; heat through.
5. To serve, pour asparagus mixture over chicken.

Each serving: About 270 calories, 38g protein, 11g carbohydrate, 9g total fat (3g saturated), 92mg cholesterol, 510mg sodium.

Chicken with Asparagus & Mushrooms

Balsamic Chicken & Pears

The unique sweet-and-sour flavor of balsamic vinegar pairs beautifully with fresh and dried fruits. Try the dish with apples and dried cranberries, too.

PREP: 10 MINUTES   COOK: 20 MINUTES
MAKES 4 MAIN-DISH SERVINGS.

2 teaspoons vegetable oil
4 small skinless, boneless chicken
  breast halves (1 pound)
2 Bosc pears, not peeled, each cut in
  half, cored, and cut into 8 wedges
1 cup chicken broth

3 tablespoons balsamic vinegar
2 teaspoons cornstarch
1 1/2 teaspoons sugar
1/4 cup dried cherries or raisins

1. In nonstick 12-inch skillet, heat 1 teaspoon oil over medium-high heat until very hot. Add chicken and cook until chicken is golden brown and loses its pink color throughout, 4 to 5 minutes per side. Transfer chicken to plate; keep warm.

2. In same skillet, heat remaining 1 teaspoon oil. Add pears and cook until tender and golden brown.

3. In cup, with fork, mix broth, vinegar, cornstarch, and sugar until well blended. Stir broth mixture and dried cherries into skillet with pears. Heat to boiling, stirring; boil 1 minute. Return chicken to skillet, and heat through.

Each serving: About 235 calories, 27g protein, 22g carbohydrate, 4g total fat (1g saturated), 66mg cholesterol, 325mg sodium.

Chicken with Grape Tomatoes

Fresh fettuccine is especially delicious and is available in the refrigerated section of most supermarkets. If you prefer, you can substitute 8 ounces dried fettuccine cooked according to package directions.

PREP: 10 MINUTES   COOK: 15 MINUTES
MAKES 2 MAIN-DISH SERVINGS.

2 teaspoons olive oil
2 medium skinless, boneless chicken breast halves (about 12 ounces)
1/4 teaspoon salt
1/4 teaspoon coarsely ground black pepper
1 package (9 ounces) fresh fettuccine

1 garlic clove, thinly sliced
1 pint grape tomatoes, each cut in half
1 cup chicken broth
1 teaspoon chopped fresh oregano leaves

1. In nonstick 10-inch skillet, heat 1 teaspoon oil over medium heat until hot. Add chicken; sprinkle with salt and pepper and cook 4 minutes. Turn chicken over and cook until golden brown, about 4 minutes longer. Transfer chicken to plate.
2. Meanwhile, in large saucepot cook fettuccine as label directs.
3. In same skillet, heat remaining 1 teaspoon oil over medium heat. Add garlic; cook, stirring, 30 seconds. Stir in tomatoes, broth, and oregano; cook 2 minutes. Return chicken to skillet; cook until juices run clear when thickest part of chicken breast is pierced with tip of knife, about 2 minutes longer.
4. To serve, drain fettuccine; divide between 2 dinner plates. Top with chicken and sauce.

Each serving: About 675 calories, 60g protein, 77g carbohydrate, 14g total fat (3g saturated), 238mg cholesterol, 970mg sodium.

New Chicken Cordon Bleu

Here's a delicious, slimmed-down version of the classic dish. We cut the fat by using part-skim mozzarella in place of Swiss cheese and served it on a bed of spinach to add extra nutrients.

PREP: 10 MINUTES   COOK: 15 MINUTES
MAKES 4 MAIN-DISH SERVINGS.

1 tablespoon butter or margarine
4 medium skinless, boneless chicken
   breast halves (1 pound)
1/2 cup chicken broth
2 tablespoons balsamic vinegar
1/8 teaspoon coarsely ground
   black pepper

4 thin slices cooked ham (about
   2 ounces)
4 thin slices part-skim mozzarella
   cheese (about 2 ounces)
1 bag (5 to 6 ounces) prewashed
   baby spinach

1. In nonstick 12-inch skillet, melt butter over medium-high heat. Add chicken breasts and cook until golden brown, about 6 minutes. Turn breasts over; cover and reduce heat to medium. Cook chicken breasts until juices run clear when thickest part of breast is pierced with tip of knife, about 6 minutes longer.

2. Increase heat to medium-high. Stir in broth, vinegar, and pepper; cook, uncovered, 1 minute. Remove skillet from heat; top each chicken breast with a slice of ham, then a slice of cheese. Cover skillet and set aside until cheese melts, about 3 minutes.

3. Arrange spinach on large platter; top with chicken breasts and drizzle with balsamic mixture.

Each serving: About 225 calories, 34g protein, 5g carbohydrate, 8g total fat (4g saturated), 90mg cholesterol, 551mg sodium.

Stuffed Chicken Breasts with Leek Sauce

For a special company entrée, fill pockets in boneless chicken breasts with prosciutto and Fontina, sauté, then serve smothered with savory leeks.

PREP: 30 MINUTES   COOK: 30 MINUTES
MAKES 4 MAIN-DISH SERVINGS.

1 small bunch leeks (about
  1 1/4 pounds)
4 medium skinless, boneless chicken
  breast halves (about 1 1/4 pounds)
4 slices prosciutto (about 2 ounces)
2 ounces Fontina cheese, cut into
  4 slices

1/4 teaspoon salt
1/4 teaspoon coarsely ground pepper
1 teaspoon olive oil
1 tablespoon butter or margarine
1/2 cup chicken broth
1/4 cup water

1. Trim roots and leaf ends from leeks. Discard any tough outer leaves. Cut each leek lengthwise in half, then thinly slice crosswise. Place leeks in large bowl of cold water; swish leeks around to remove any sand. With hand, transfer leeks to colander. Repeat process, changing water several times, until all sand is removed. Drain well.

2. With knife, cut each chicken breast half parallel to its surface to form a deep pocket with a small opening. Place equal portions of prosciutto and Fontina in each pocket, cutting to fit if necessary; press chicken to seal in filling. Sprinkle chicken with salt and pepper.

3. In nonstick 12-inch skillet, heat oil over medium-high heat until hot. Add chicken and cook 3 minutes per side. Reduce heat to medium-low; cover and cook until juices run clear when thickest part of breast is pierced with tip of knife, 6 to 8 minutes longer. Transfer chicken to platter; keep warm.

4. In same skillet, melt butter over medium heat. Add leeks and cook, stirring frequently, until tender and golden, 10 to 12 minutes. Add broth and water; heat to boiling over medium-high heat. Boil until slightly reduced, about 2 minutes.

5. To serve, pour leek sauce over chicken.

Each serving: About 325 calories, 42g protein, 10g carbohydrate, 13g total fat (6g saturated), 116mg cholesterol, 821mg sodium.

Weeknight Country Captain

Legend has it that this delicious curried chicken, which has been popular in the South for decades, got its name from a British army officer who brought the recipe back from his station in India. But some food historians believe the recipe originated in Savannah, once a major shipping port for the spice trade. Typically made with cut-up chicken, we've streamlined it for an easy weeknight dinner by calling for chicken tenders.

PREP: 25 MINUTES   COOK: 30 MINUTES
MAKES 6 MAIN-DISH SERVINGS.

2 tablespoons all-purpose flour
2 tablespoons curry powder
1 1/2 pounds chicken breast tenders
4 teaspoons olive oil
1 jumbo onion (1 pound), chopped
1 medium green pepper, chopped
1 medium Granny Smith apple, peeled, cored, and cut into 1/4-inch pieces
2 garlic cloves, crushed with garlic press

1 tablespoon grated, peeled fresh ginger
3/4 teaspoon salt
1 can (14 1/2 ounces) whole tomatoes in juice
3/4 cup chicken broth
1/2 cup dark seedless raisins
1/4 cup almonds, toasted and coarsely chopped
hot cooked rice

1. Combine flour and 1 tablespoon curry powder in large ziptight plastic bag. Add chicken tenders and toss to coat well.

2. In deep nonstick 12-inch skillet, heat 2 teaspoons oil over medium-high heat until hot. Add chicken tenders and cook until browned, about 4 minutes per side. Transfer chicken to plate; set aside.

3. In same skillet, heat remaining 2 teaspoons oil until hot. Add onion, green pepper, and apple and cook, stirring often, until vegetables are tender, about 10 minutes.

4. Stir in garlic, ginger, salt, and remaining 1 tablespoon curry powder; cook, stirring, 1 minute. Add tomatoes with their juice and broth, breaking up tomatoes with side of spoon; heat to boiling.

5. Return chicken to skillet. Reduce heat to low; cover and simmer until chicken loses its pink color throughout, about 8 minutes. Stir in raisins and sprinkle with almonds. Serve with hot cooked rice.

Each serving without rice: About 305 calories, 30g protein, 29g carbohydrate, 8g total fat (1g saturated), 66g cholesterol, 595mg sodium.

Weeknight Country Captain

Skillet Arroz Con Pollo

Skillet Arroz Con Pollo

This dish, popular in Spain and Mexico, literally means "rice with chicken." We call for chicken breast tenders instead of bone-in pieces to shorten cooking time.

PREP: 15 MINUTES   COOK: 40 MINUTES
MAKES 4 MAIN-DISH SERVINGS.

1 tablespoon olive oil
1 medium onion, finely chopped
1 medium red pepper, cut into
   1/2-inch pieces
1 cup regular long-grain white rice
1 garlic clove, minced
1/8 teaspoon ground red pepper
   (cayenne)
1 strip (3'' by 1/2'') lemon peel
1/4 teaspoon salt
1 can (14 1/2 ounces) chicken broth

1/4 cup dry sherry or water
1 pound chicken breast tenders, cut
   into 2-inch pieces
1 cup frozen peas
1/4 cup chopped pimiento-stuffed
   olives (salad olives), drained
1/2 cup loosely packed fresh cilantro
   or parsley leaves, chopped
lemon wedges

1. In nonstick 12-inch skillet, heat oil over medium heat until hot. Add onion and red pepper, and cook, stirring occasionally, until tender, about 12 minutes. Stir in rice, garlic, and ground red pepper; cook 2 minutes. Stir in lemon peel, salt, chicken broth, and sherry; heat to boiling over medium-high heat. Reduce heat to low; cover and simmer 13 minutes.
2. Stir in chicken tenders; cover and simmer, stirring once halfway through cooking time, until juices run clear when chicken is pierced with tip of knife and rice is tender, about 13 minutes longer. Stir in frozen peas; cover and heat through. Remove skillet from heat; let stand 5 minutes.
3. Stir in olives, and sprinkle with cilantro. Serve with lemon wedges.

Each serving: About 410 calories, 34g protein, 49g carbohydrate, 7g total fat (2g saturated), 66mg cholesterol, 925mg sodium.

Pan-Browned Chicken & Artichokes

First we tried this low-fat sauté with frozen artichoke hearts, but they were too bland; then with marinated ones, which were too acidic. In our third test, we used the canned kind, which had the best texture and flavor.

PREP: 20 MINUTES   COOK: 10 MINUTES
MAKES 4 MAIN-DISH SERVINGS.

1 tablespoon olive oil
1 pound chicken breast tenders,
  cut into bite-size pieces
1/4 teaspoon salt
1/4 teaspoon coarsely ground
  black pepper
1 garlic clove, crushed with
  garlic press

1/2 cup chicken broth
1 teaspoon cornstarch
1/2 teaspoon freshly grated
  lemon peel
1 can (14 ounces) artichoke hearts,
  rinsed, drained, and each cut in half
1 pint grape tomatoes or
  cherry tomatoes

1. In nonstick 12-inch skillet, heat olive oil over medium-high heat until hot. Add chicken; sprinkle with salt and pepper. Cook, stirring often, until chicken is lightly browned, about 5 minutes.

2. Meanwhile, in cup, with fork, mix garlic, broth, cornstarch, and grated lemon peel.

3. To chicken in skillet, add artichokes, tomatoes, and broth mixture; heat to boiling, stirring. Boil 1 minute.

Each serving: About 195 calories, 29g protein, 8g carbohydrate, 5g total fat (1g saturated), 66mg cholesterol, 500mg sodium.

Pan-Browned Chicken & Artichokes

Couscous Paella

Couscous Paella

A box of couscous makes paella quick enough for a weeknight supper. Serve with a salad blend from the supermarket tossed with your favorite vinaigrette dressing.

PREP: 10 MINUTES COOK: 10 MINUTES
MAKES 4 MAIN-DISH SERVINGS.

1 can (14 1/2 ounces) chicken broth
1/4 cup water
1 package (10 ounces) couscous
  (Moroccan pasta)
1 package (10 ounces) frozen peas
2 teaspoons olive oil
1 red or green pepper, chopped
2 ounces low-fat kielbasa (smoked
  Polish sausage), cut into
  1/4-inch slices
12 ounces skinless, boneless
  chicken breast, cut into
  1-inch pieces

1 garlic clove, crushed with
  garlic press
1/2 teaspoon salt
1/4 teaspoon coarsely ground
  black pepper
1/4 teaspoon dried thyme leaves
1 1/2 cups cherry tomatoes, each
  cut in half

1. In 3-quart saucepan, heat broth and water to boiling over high heat. Remove saucepan from heat; stir in couscous and frozen peas. Cover saucepan and let stand 5 minutes, or until ready to use.
2. Meanwhile, in nonstick 12-inch skillet, heat oil over medium-high heat until hot. Add red or green pepper and kielbasa and cook, stirring occasionally, 5 minutes. Add chicken, garlic, salt, black pepper, and thyme, and cook, stirring occasionally, until chicken loses its pink color through-out, about 5 minutes. Remove skillet from heat, and stir in cherry tomatoes.
3. Fluff couscous with fork; add to chicken mixture in skillet, and toss gently to combine.

Each serving: About 520 calories, 38g protein, 73g carbohydrate, 8g total fat (1g saturated), 50mg cholesterol, 725mg sodium.

Skillet Chicken Parmesan

We sautéed thinly sliced chicken breasts in just a teaspoon of olive oil and used part-skim mozzarella to lighten up this family favorite. Ready-made spaghetti sauce makes this a great weeknight recipe.

PREP: 10 MINUTES   COOK: 10 MINUTES
MAKES 4 MAIN-DISH SERVINGS.

1 teaspoon olive oil
1 pound skinless, boneless chicken breasts, thinly sliced
1 container (15 ounces) refrigerated marinara sauce
1 cup shredded part-skim mozzarella cheese (4 ounces)

2 plum tomatoes, chopped
2 tablespoons freshly grated Parmesan cheese
1 cup loosely packed fresh basil leaves, sliced

1. In nonstick 12-inch skillet, heat oil over medium-high heat until hot. Add half of chicken to skillet, and cook until browned on both sides and just cooked through, about 2 minutes per side. Transfer cooked chicken to plate; repeat with remaining chicken.

2. Reduce heat to medium. Return chicken to skillet; top with marinara sauce and mozzarella. Cover and cook until sauce is heated through and the mozzarella has melted, about 2 minutes. Sprinkle with tomatoes, Parmesan, and basil.

Each serving: About 295 calories, 36g protein, 10g carbohydrate, 11g total fat (4g saturated), 84mg cholesterol, 660mg sodium.

Asian Stir-Fry with Spring Peas

Serve over fluffy white rice for a simple and flavorful supper.

PREP: 20 MINUTES   COOK: 20 MINUTES
MAKES 4 MAIN-DISH SERVINGS.

1 pound chicken breast tenders
1/2 teaspoon Chinese five-spice
   powder
1/4 teaspoon salt
3 teaspoons vegetable oil
8 ounces snow peas and/or sugar
   snap peas, strings removed
2 tablespoons water
1 medium red pepper, thinly sliced
1 cup chicken broth

1 tablespoon dark brown sugar
1 tablespoon soy sauce
2 tablespoons cornstarch
2 green onions, trimmed and cut into
   1/2-inch pieces
1 tablespoon grated, peeled
   fresh ginger
2 garlic cloves, crushed with
   garlic press

1. On waxed paper, sprinkle chicken with Chinese five-spice powder and salt. In nonstick 12-inch skillet, heat 1 teaspoon oil over medium-high heat until hot. Add chicken and cook just until it loses its pink color throughout, about 2 1/2 minutes per side. Transfer to plate; set aside.

2. In same skillet, heat remaining 2 teaspoons oil until hot. Add peas and red pepper and cook, stirring occasionally, until golden, about 5 minutes. Add water and cook, covered, stirring occasionally, until vegetables are tender-crisp, about 3 minutes.

3. Meanwhile, in measuring cup, whisk broth, brown sugar, soy sauce, and cornstarch until smooth.

4. Add green onions, ginger, and garlic to skillet; cook, stirring, 1 minute. Stir broth mixture, then add to skillet; heat to boiling. Boil 30 seconds. Add chicken and heat through.

Each serving: About 220 calories, 30g protein, 12g carbohydrate, 5g total fat (1g saturated), 66mg cholesterol, 665mg sodium.

Thai Chicken with Basil

A fragrant blend of cool and hot flavors lends an exotic touch to this stir-fry.

Prep: 20 minutes plus marinating   Cook: 10 minutes
Makes 4 main-dish servings.

1 pound skinless, boneless chicken
breast halves
3 tablespoons Asian fish sauce
(nuoc nam, see Tip below)
1 tablespoon soy sauce
1 tablespoon brown sugar
2 teaspoons vegetable oil
1 large onion (12 ounces), cut into
1/4-inch-thick slices

2 red or green chiles (serrano or
jalapeño), seeded and cut into
matchstick strips
2 teaspoons minced, peeled
fresh ginger
2 garlic cloves, crushed with
garlic press
1 1/2 cups loosely packed fresh
basil leaves

1. With knife held in slanting position, almost parallel to cutting surface, cut each chicken breast half crosswise into 1/4-inch-thick slices. In medium bowl, combine fish sauce, soy sauce, and brown sugar; add chicken slices, tossing to coat. Let marinate 5 minutes.

2. In nonstick 12-inch skillet, heat oil over medium-high heat until very hot. Add chicken with marinade and cook, stirring frequently (stir-frying), until chicken loses its pink color throughout, 3 to 4 minutes. With slotted spoon, transfer chicken to bowl.

3. Add onion to marinade remaining in skillet and cook (stir-frying) until tender-crisp, about 4 minutes. Stir in chiles, ginger, and garlic; cook 1 minute.

4. Return chicken to skillet; heat through. Stir in basil leaves just before serving.

Each serving: About 238 calories, 31g protein, 6g carbohydrate, 5g total fat (1g saturated), 66mg cholesterol, 784mg sodium.

Tip

Asian fish sauce (nuoc nam or nam pla) is available in specialty sections of some supermarkets or in Asian groceries.

Thai Chicken with Basil

Szechuan Chicken

Dry-roasted peanuts add crunch to this spicy Chinese-style supper. Serve it over rice or Asian rice noodles.

PREP: 20 MINUTES   COOK: 10 MINUTES
MAKES 4 MAIN-DISH SERVINGS.

1 pound skinless, boneless chicken breast halves
2 tablespoons soy sauce
2 tablespoons dry sherry
2 teaspoons cornstarch
2 teaspoons grated, peeled fresh ginger
1/4 teaspoon sugar
1/4 teaspoon crushed red pepper

2 tablespoons vegetable oil
6 green onions, trimmed and cut into 2-inch pieces
1 green pepper, cut into 1/2-inch pieces
1 red pepper, cut into 1/2-inch pieces
1/4 cup dry-roasted unsalted peanuts

1. With knife held in slanting position, almost parallel to cutting surface, cut each chicken breast half crosswise into 1/8-inch-thick slices. In medium bowl, combine soy sauce, sherry, cornstarch, ginger, sugar, and crushed red pepper; add chicken, tossing to coat.

2. In 12-inch skillet, heat 1 tablespoon oil over medium-high heat until very hot. Add green onions and green and red peppers, and cook, stirring frequently (stir-frying), until vegetables are tender-crisp, 2 to 3 minutes. With slotted spoon, transfer vegetables to bowl.

3. Increase heat to high and add remaining 1 tablespoon oil to skillet; heat until very hot. Add chicken mixture, and stir-fry until chicken loses its pink color throughout, 2 to 3 minutes. Return vegetables to skillet; heat mixture through.

4. To serve, transfer chicken and vegetables to warm platter and sprinkle with peanuts.

Each serving: About 277 calories, 30g protein, 9g carbohydrate, 13g total fat (2g saturated), 66mg cholesterol, 594mg sodium.

Tarragon-Mushroom Turkey Cutlets

Cream of mushroom soup is an instant sauce for this easy skillet recipe. Great over noodles or braised greens.

PREP: 10 MINUTES   COOK: 10 MINUTES
MAKES 4 MAIN-DISH SERVINGS.

2 teaspoons olive oil
4 turkey-breast cutlets (about
   4 ounces each)
1 shallot, finely chopped
1 package (4 ounces) assorted
   sliced wild mushrooms
1/3 cup dry white wine

1 can (15 to 19 ounces) condensed
   cream of mushroom soup
1 tablespoon chopped fresh
   tarragon leaves
1/4 teaspoon ground black pepper
1/3 cup water

1. In nonstick 10-inch skillet, heat oil over medium-high heat until hot. Add cutlets and cook, until they just lose their pink color throughout, 2 to 3 minutes per side. Transfer cutlets to plate; keep warm.

2. Reduce heat to medium. Add shallot and mushrooms to skillet; cook until browned and tender, about 3 minutes. Add wine; heat to boiling. Boil 1 minute. Stir in undiluted soup, tarragon, pepper, and water; heat to boiling. Return cutlets with any juices in plate to skillet; heat through, turning to coat.

Each serving: About 305 calories, 32g protein, 13g carbohydrate, 13g total fat (3g saturated), 72mg cholesterol, 1,000mg sodium.

Turkey & White Bean Chili

Here's a low-fat chili that's full of flavor. If you prefer, substitute ground chicken for the ground turkey.

PREP: 8 MINUTES   COOK: 15 MINUTES
MAKES 4 MAIN-DISH SERVINGS.

1 tablespoon olive oil
1 medium onion, chopped
1 pound ground turkey
2 teaspoons ground coriander
2 teaspoons ground cumin
2 teaspoons fresh thyme leaves
2 cans (15 to 19 ounces each) Great Northern beans, rinsed and drained

1 can (4 to 4 1/2 ounces) chopped mild green chiles
1 can (14 1/2 ounces) chicken broth
2 small tomatoes (about 4 ounces each), coarsely chopped
1 lime, cut into wedges

1. In nonstick 12-inch skillet, heat oil over medium-high heat until hot. Add onion and cook, stirring frequently, until tender and golden, about 5 minutes. Add turkey and cook, breaking up turkey with side of spoon, until it loses its pink color throughout, about 5 minutes. Stir in coriander, cumin, and thyme; cook 1 minute.

2. Meanwhile, in small bowl, mash half of beans.

3. Add mashed and whole beans, undrained chiles, and broth to turkey mixture; heat to boiling over medium-high heat. Boil until chili thickens slightly, about 1 minute. Stir in chopped tomatoes; heat through. Serve with lime wedges.

Each serving: About 495 calories, 35g protein, 49g carbohydrate, 18g total fat (4g saturated), 90mg cholesterol, 1,040mg sodium.

Turkey Marsala with Mushrooms

Turkey cutlets are an excellent and economical substitute for veal scallopini, and this recipe proves it.

PREP: 15 MINUTES   COOK: 15 MINUTES
MAKES 4 MAIN-DISH SERVINGS.

2 tablespoons butter or margarine
10 ounces mushrooms, trimmed
  and sliced
3/4 teaspoon salt
1 pound turkey cutlets, large pieces
  cut in half

3 tablespoons all-purpose flour
1/4 teaspoon ground black pepper
1 tablespoon olive oil
1/2 cup dry Marsala wine
1/4 cup water

1. In nonstick 12-inch skillet, melt 1 tablespoon butter over medium-high heat. Add mushrooms and 1/4 teaspoon salt; cook until mushrooms are golden brown and liquid has evaporated, about 7 minutes. With slotted spoon, transfer mushrooms to medium bowl.

2. Meanwhile, with meat mallet or between two sheets of plastic wrap or waxed paper with rolling pin, pound turkey cutlets to 1/4-inch thickness. On waxed paper, combine flour, pepper, and remaining 1/2 teaspoon salt; use to coat cutlets, shaking off excess.

3. In same skillet, melt remaining 1 tablespoon butter with oil over medium-high heat. Add half of cutlets and cook until cutlets are golden brown and lose their pink color throughout, 1 to 2 minutes per side. Transfer cutlets to bowl with mushrooms; keep warm. Repeat with remaining cutlets.

4. To skillet, add Marsala and water; cook 1 minute. Stir in turkey cutlets and mushrooms, turning to coat with sauce.

Each serving: About 284 calories, 30g protein, 9g carbohydrate, 10g total fat (4g saturated), 86mg cholesterol, 556mg sodium.

Spicy Turkey Chili

Spicy Turkey Chili

Serve this winter-white chili (no tomato!) with fluffy rice, salad, and Italian bread.

PREP: 5 MINUTES   COOK: 15 MINUTES
MAKES 6 MAIN-DISH SERVINGS.

1 teaspoon olive oil
1 pound ground turkey breast
1 small onion, diced
1 teaspoon ground coriander
1 teaspoon ground cumin
1/4 teaspoon salt
2 cans (15 to 16 ounces each) no-salt-added navy or small white beans, rinsed and drained

1 can (14 1/2 ounces) reduced-sodium chicken broth
1 package (10 ounces) frozen whole-kernel corn, thawed
1 can (4 to 4 1/2 ounces) chopped mild green chiles, drained
2 tablespoons cayenne pepper sauce (see Tip below)
1 cup chopped fresh cilantro leaves

1. In nonstick 12-inch skillet, heat oil over medium-high heat until hot. Add ground turkey and onion; cook, stirring and breaking up meat with side of spoon, until meat loses its pink color and liquid has evaporated, about 10 minutes. Add coriander, cumin, and salt; cook, stirring to combine, 1 minute.

2. Meanwhile, in small bowl, mash half of beans; set aside.

3. Add mashed and unmashed beans, broth, corn, and chiles to turkey mixture. Heat to boiling over medium-high heat; stir in pepper sauce. Sprinkle chili with cilantro.

Each serving: About 270 calories, 28g protein, 33g carbohydrate, 3g total fat (1g saturated), 45mg cholesterol, 825mg sodium.

Tip

Cayenne pepper sauce is a milder variety of hot pepper sauce that adds tang, flavor, and a lower dose of heat.

Kielbasa & Sauerkraut Medley

A hearty one-skillet dinner made with apples, carrots, and red potatoes.

PREP: 15 MINUTES   COOK: 25 MINUTES
MAKES 4 MAIN-DISH SERVINGS.

8 ounces reduced-fat turkey kielbasa, cut diagonally into 1/2-inch-thick slices
12 ounces red potatoes, cut into 1-inch chunks
2 cups shredded carrots (about half 10-ounce bag)

1 bag (16 ounces) sauerkraut, rinsed and drained
2 Golden Delicious apples, unpeeled, cored, and cut into 1/2-inch chunks
1/3 cup water

1. Heat nonstick 12-inch skillet over medium-high heat until hot. Add kielbasa and cook, stirring occasionally, until golden, 3 to 4 minutes.
2. Add potatoes, carrots, sauerkraut, apples, and water; heat to boiling. Reduce heat to medium-low; cover and simmer until potatoes are fork-tender, 18 to 20 minutes.

Each serving: About 230 calories, 11g protein, 40g carbohydrate, 5g total fat (2g saturated), 35mg cholesterol, 935mg sodium.

Kielbasa & Sauerkraut Medley

MEAT

Tuscan Beef with Spinach
recipe on page 69

Italian Steak and Beans

Italian Steak & Beans

This hearty Italian-style meal can be fixed in a flash—perfect when time and energy are in short supply.

PREP: 5 MINUTES   COOK: 15 MINUTES
MAKES 4 MAIN-DISH SERVINGS.

1 teaspoon olive oil
2 boneless beef strip or rib-eye
   steaks, 3/4 inch thick (about
   10 ounces each), trimmed
1/2 teaspoon salt
1/2 teaspoon coarsely ground pepper
1 medium onion, sliced
1/3 cup balsamic vinegar

2 teaspoons chopped fresh rosemary
2 tablespoons water
1 pint grape or cherry tomatoes
1 can (15 to 19 ounces) white
   kidney beans (cannellini),
   rinsed and drained

1. In 10-inch skillet, heat oil over medium-high heat until very hot but not smoking. Sprinkle steaks with salt and pepper. Add steaks to skillet, and cook, for medium-rare, 4 to 5 minutes per side, or until desired doneness. Transfer steaks to cutting board; keep warm.

2. Reduce heat to medium. Add onion to drippings in skillet, and cook, stirring, until browned and tender, about 5 minutes. Add vinegar, rosemary, and water, stirring until browned bits are loosened from bottom of skillet. Stir in tomatoes and beans; cook, stirring occasionally, until heated through, about 2 minutes.

3. Thinly slice steaks, and serve with tomato-and-bean mixture.

Each serving: About 495 calories, 35g protein, 29g carbohydrate, 25g total fat (10g saturated), 76mg cholesterol, 540mg sodium.

Pan-Fried Steaks with Spinach & Tomatoes

Juicy top loin steaks topped with a garlicky lemon rub are complemented by quickly sautéed vegetables.

PREP: 15 MINUTES   COOK: 15 MINUTES
MAKES 4 MAIN-DISH SERVINGS.

1 large garlic clove, crushed with
  garlic press
1 teaspoon freshly grated lemon peel
1/2 teaspoon salt
1/2 teaspoon coarsely ground
  black pepper
1 teaspoon olive oil
2 boneless beef top loin or rib-eye
  steaks, 3/4 inch thick (10 ounces
  each), trimmed

1/2 cup chicken broth
1 teaspoon cornstarch
1 cup grape tomatoes or cherry
  tomatoes, each cut in half
1 bag (10 ounces) prewashed
  spinach, tough stems trimmed

1. In cup, with fork, blend garlic, lemon peel, salt, and pepper. Spread garlic mixture on both sides of steaks.

2. In nonstick 12-inch skillet, heat oil over medium heat until hot. Add steaks and cook for medium-rare, 5 to 6 minutes per side, or until desired doneness. Transfer steaks to plate; keep warm.

3. In cup, mix broth and cornstarch. To same skillet, add broth mixture, tomatoes, and spinach. Heat to boiling over medium-high heat and cook, stirring, until spinach wilts, 1 to 2 minutes. Cut each steak in half; serve with spinach mixture.

Each serving: About 350 calories, 30g protein, 3g carbohydrate, 24g total fat (9g saturated), 92mg cholesterol, 540mg sodium.

Pan-Fried Steaks with Spinach & Tomatoes

Beef Pizzaiola

Serve our tender, Italian-style steaks with a loaf of hot crusty bread to soak up the luscious tomato pan sauce.

<small>PREP: 15 MINUTES   COOK: 25 MINUTES
MAKES 4 MAIN-DISH SERVINGS.</small>

2 boneless beef top loin steaks, 3/4 inch thick (10 ounces each), trimmed
1/2 teaspoon salt
1/4 teaspoon coarsely ground black pepper
1 tablespoon olive oil
1 large onion (12 ounces), cut in half and sliced
1 small red pepper, cut into 1-inch pieces
1 small green pepper, cut into 1-inch pieces
2 garlic cloves, crushed with garlic press
1/2 cup chicken broth
2 tablespoons red wine vinegar
1 teaspoon sugar
8 cherry tomatoes, each cut in half
1/2 cup lightly packed fresh basil leaves, chopped

1. Pat steaks dry with paper towels. Sprinkle steaks with 1/4 teaspoon salt and pepper.

2. Heat nonstick 12-inch skillet over medium-high until hot. Add steaks and cook about 4 minutes per side for medium-rare, or until desired doneness. Transfer steaks to platter; keep warm.

3. In same skillet, heat oil over medium heat until hot. Add onion, red and green peppers, garlic, and remaining 1/4 teaspoon salt; cook, stirring often, until vegetables are tender and golden, about 10 minutes.

4. Increase heat to medium-high. Stir in broth, red wine vinegar, sugar, and tomatoes; heat to boiling. Cook 1 minute. Remove skillet from heat, and stir in basil.

5. To serve, slice steaks and arrange on 4 dinner plates; top steaks with the pepper mixture.

Each serving: About 315 calories, 32g protein, 16g carbohydrate, 13g total fat (4g saturated), 88mg cholesterol, 450 mg sodium.

Beef Pizzaiola

Tuscan Beef with Spinach

Tuscan Beef with Spinach

Northern Italy, especially Tuscany, is known for its fine beef. Here, tender top loin steaks are paired with two other Italian favorites—spinach and white kidney beans—to make a spectacular stovetop supper.

PREP: 15 MINUTES   COOK: 15 MINUTES
MAKES 4 MAIN-DISH SERVINGS.

2 boneless beef top loin steaks,
 3/4 inch thick (10 ounces each)
 trimmed
1/2 teaspoon salt
1 tablespoon olive oil
2 garlic cloves, minced
1 can (15 to 19 ounces) white
 kidney beans (cannellini),
 rinsed and drained

1/2 teaspoon dried rosemary, crushed
1/4 teaspoon crushed red pepper
1/2 cup chicken broth
1 pound fresh spinach, washed,
 dried, and tough stems trimmed

1. Pat steaks dry with paper towels. Sprinkle steaks with 1/4 teaspoon salt.
2. Heat nonstick 12-inch skillet over medium-high heat until hot. Add steaks and cook about 4 minutes per side for medium-rare, or until desired doneness. Transfer steaks to platter; keep warm.
3. Reduce heat to low. To same skillet, add oil and garlic and cook, stirring, about 30 seconds. Stir in beans, rosemary, red pepper, and remaining 1/4 teaspoon salt; cook 1 minute. Add broth; heat to boiling over medium-high heat. Gradually add spinach, stirring, until spinach just wilts, about 2 minutes longer.
4. To serve, slice steaks and arrange on 4 dinner plates; top with bean-and-spinach mixture.

Each serving: About 380 calories, 40g protein, 24g carbohydrate, 14g total fat (4g saturated), 88mg cholesterol, 800mg sodium.

Korean Steak in Lettuce Cups

Sliced round steak and shredded carrots are braised in a rich soy–ginger sauce and served in delicate Boston lettuce leaves.

PREP: 15 MINUTES PLUS MARINATING   COOK: 6 MINUTES
MAKES 4 MAIN-DISH SERVINGS.

3 tablespoons soy sauce
1 tablespoon sugar
2 teaspoons Asian sesame oil
1 teaspoon minced, peeled
   fresh ginger
1/4 teaspoon ground red pepper
   (cayenne)
1 garlic clove, crushed with garlic
   press
1 beef top round steak (about
   1 pound), trimmed and cut into
   1/2-inch cubes

4 stalks celery with leaves,
   thinly sliced
1/2 (10-ounce) package shredded
   carrots (1 3/4 cups)
1/3 cup water
3 green onions, trimmed and
   thinly sliced
1 tablespoon sesame seeds
1 head Boston lettuce, separated
   into leaves
green-onion tops

1. In medium bowl, stir soy sauce, sugar, oil, ginger, ground red pepper, and garlic until blended. Add beef, turning to coat with soy-sauce mixture, and marinate, stirring occasionally, 15 minutes at room temperature.

2. In nonstick 12-inch skillet, heat celery, carrots, and water to boiling over medium-high heat. Cook, stirring occasionally, until vegetables are tender-crisp, 2 to 3 minutes. Add beef and marinade, and cook, stirring frequently (stir-frying), until meat just loses its pink color throughout, about 2 minutes. Stir in green onions and sesame seeds, and cook, stirring, 1 minute.

3. To serve, let each person place some beef mixture on a lettuce leaf. Garnish with green-onion tops. If you like, fold sides of lettuce leaf over filling to make a package to eat out of hand.

Each serving: About 250 calories, 28g protein, 12g carbohydrate, 10g total fat (3g saturated), 53mg cholesterol, 855mg sodium.

Korean Steak in Lettuce Cups

Beef Stew with Red Wine

Beef Stew with Red Wine

Precooked beef roast makes this hearty stew a snap to prepare.

PREP: 5 MINUTES   COOK: 15 MINUTES
MAKES 4 MAIN-DISH SERVINGS.

1 pound red potatoes (about 4
   medium), cut into 1-inch chunks
2 teaspoons vegetable oil
2 large garlic cloves, sliced
1 medium onion, cut into
   1-inch pieces
1 bag (10 ounces) stringless snap
   pea and carrot blend

1/4 cup water
1/2 cup dry red wine
1 package (17 ounces) fully cooked
   beef roast au jus, cut into 1-inch
   pieces, and juices reserved
1/8 teaspoon ground black pepper

1. Place potatoes in microwave-safe pie plate or medium bowl. Cook in microwave oven on High until fork-tender, about 4 minutes.

2. Meanwhile, in 12-inch skillet, heat oil over medium heat. Add garlic and onion, and cook until tender and lightly browned, about 5 minutes. Add snap peas and carrots and water; cover and cook, stirring occasionally, until carrots are tender, 5 to 6 minutes. Add wine; boil 1 minute.

3. Stir in beef with its juices and pepper, and cook until heated through, about 2 minutes. Gently stir in potatoes just before serving.

Each serving: About 340 calories, 28g protein, 35g carbohydrate, 10g total fat (4g saturated), 64mg cholesterol, 415mg sodium.

Beef & Barley with Mushrooms

A satisfying dinner of sautéed beef tossed with a rich barley-and-mushroom pilaf. Because top round steak is a very lean cut, it must be thinly sliced across the grain; otherwise it may be tough.

PREP: 25 MINUTES   COOK: 50 MINUTES

MAKES 6 MAIN-DISH SERVINGS.

3 cups boiling water
1 package (1/2 ounce) dried porcini mushrooms (about 1/2 cup)
1 beef top round steak, 3/4 inch thick (about 12 ounces)
1 teaspoon olive oil
1 tablespoon soy sauce
1 package (8 ounces) sliced white mushrooms
2 medium carrots, peeled and cut lengthwise in half, then crosswise into 1/4-inch-thick slices

1 medium onion, finely chopped
1/2 teaspoon salt
1/4 teaspoon ground black pepper
1/4 teaspoon dried thyme
1 1/2 cups pearl barley (about 10 ounces)
1 can (14 1/2 ounces) chicken broth
1/2 cup loosely packed fresh parsley leaves

1. In medium bowl, pour boiling water over porcini; let stand 10 minutes.
2. Meanwhile, cut steak lengthwise in half. With knife held in slanting position, almost parallel to cutting surface, cut each half of steak crosswise into 1/8-inch-thick slices.
3. In deep nonstick 12-inch skillet, heat oil over medium-high heat until very hot. Add half of steak slices; cook, stirring frequently (stir-frying), until steak just loses its pink color, about 2 minutes. Transfer steak to medium bowl; repeat with remaining steak. Toss steak with soy sauce; set aside.
4. To same skillet, add white mushrooms, carrots, onion, salt, pepper, and thyme, and cook over medium-high heat, stirring occasionally, until vegetables are tender-crisp, about 10 minutes.
5. Meanwhile, with slotted spoon, remove porcini from soaking liquid, reserving liquid. Rinse porcini and coarsely chop. Strain soaking liquid through sieve lined with paper towel into medium bowl.
6. Add barley, broth, porcini, and soaking liquid to vegetables in skillet; heat mixture to boiling over medium-high heat. Reduce heat to medium-

Beef & Barley with Mushrooms

low; cover and simmer, stirring occasionally, until barley and vegetables are tender and most of liquid has evaporated, 35 to 40 minutes. Stir in steak mixture and parsley; heat through.

Each serving: About 320 calories, 20g protein, 47g carbohydrate, 7g total fat (2g saturated), 34mg cholesterol, 695mg sodium.

Stroganoff Steaks

The classic sour cream and mushroom sauce is traditionally served on sliced beef. But we discovered it's delicious over pan-fried steaks, too.

PREP: 10 MINUTES   COOK: 15 MINUTES
MAKES 4 MAIN-DISH SERVINGS.

SKILLET STEAKS
4 beef cubed steaks (about
    4 ounces each)
1/4 teaspoon salt
1/4 teaspoon coarsely ground
    black pepper
2 teaspoons vegetable oil

STROGANOFF SAUCE
1 teaspoon vegetable oil
10 ounces white mushrooms,
    trimmed and sliced

1 small onion, finely chopped
1/2 cup chicken broth
1/4 cup reduced-fat sour cream
1/2 teaspoon Dijon mustard
1/8 teaspoon coarsely ground
    black pepper
1 tablespoon chopped fresh dill

1. Prepare Skillet Steaks: Pat steaks dry with paper towels. Sprinkle steaks with salt and pepper.

2. In nonstick 12-inch skillet, heat oil over medium-high heat until hot. Add steaks, and cook 5 to 6 minutes for medium, turning steaks over once. When steaks are done, transfer to platter with any juice; cover with foil to keep warm.

3. Prepare Stroganoff Sauce: In same skillet, heat oil over medium-high heat until hot. Add mushrooms and onion, and cook, stirring occasionally, until onion is tender and all liquid has evaporated, about 8 minutes. Add broth; heat to boiling. Boil until slightly reduced, about 1 minute. Remove skillet from heat; stir in sour cream, mustard, pepper, and dill.

4. Return steaks with their juice to skillet; heat through.

Each serving: About 315 calories, 26g protein, 6g carbohydrate, 20g total fat (6g saturated), 77mg cholesterol, 320mg sodium.

Beef & Pepper Fajitas

These are great for a casual dinner party—just double everything for eight. The secret for speed: prepackaged sliced meat.

PREP: 15 MINUTES   COOK: 25 MINUTES
MAKES 4 MAIN-DISH SERVINGS.

4 teaspoons vegetable oil
1 medium red pepper, thinly sliced
1 medium green pepper, thinly sliced
1 medium onion, thinly sliced
1 tablespoon chili powder
1 teaspoon ground cumin
3/4 teaspoon salt
1/4 teaspoon ground red pepper
    (cayenne)

1 pound sliced beef for stir-fry or
    flank steak, thinly sliced
4 (10-inch) flour tortillas, warmed
accompaniments: fresh cilantro
    leaves, sliced avocado, jarred
    salsa, sour cream

1. In nonstick 12-inch skillet, heat 2 teaspoons oil over medium heat until hot. Add red and green peppers and onion, and cook, stirring occasionally, until tender and lightly browned, about 20 minutes. Transfer vegetable mixture to plate; set aside.

2. Meanwhile, in medium bowl, mix chili powder, cumin, salt, and ground red pepper. Add beef and toss until evenly coated.

3. In same skillet, heat 1 teaspoon oil over medium-high heat. Add half of seasoned beef, and cook, stirring, until beef just loses its pink color, about 2 minutes. Transfer beef to plate with vegetables. Repeat with remaining 1 teaspoon oil and beef.

4. Return vegetable mixture and beef to skillet; toss until mixed. Serve in warm tortillas with accompaniments.

Each serving without accompaniments: About 435 calories, 31g protein, 38g carbohydrate, 18g total fat (5g saturated), 46mg cholesterol, 765mg sodium.

Tangerine Beef Stir-fry

Tangerine Beef Stir-Fry

Here's a delicious, lightened-up version of the ever-popular Chinese take-out dish. Serve with steamed rice.

PREP: 20 MINUTES   COOK: 15 MINUTES
MAKES 4 MAIN-DISH SERVINGS.

2 to 3 tangerines (about
  1$^{1}/_{2}$ pounds)
$^{1}/_{4}$ cup dry sherry
2 tablespoons hoisin sauce
2 tablespoons cornstarch
2 tablespoons soy sauce
1 beef flank steak (about 1 pound),
  cut crosswise into $^{1}/_{8}$-inch-thick
  slices

5 teaspoons vegetable oil
1 bag (12 ounces) broccoli flowerets
1 medium red pepper, thinly sliced
1 tablespoon grated, peeled
  fresh ginger

1. Cut peel from 1 tangerine. With small knife, remove any white pith from peel; cut peel into very thin slices, and set aside. Holding tangerines over measuring cups, squeeze $^{1}/_{2}$ cup juice. Stir in sherry and hoisin sauce; set aside. In medium bowl, combine cornstarch, soy sauce, and steak; set aside.

2. In nonstick 12-inch skillet, heat 1 teaspoon oil over medium-high heat until very hot. Add broccoli, red pepper, ginger, and peel to skillet; cook, stirring frequently (stir-frying), until vegetables are tender-crisp, about 3 minutes. Transfer to large bowl.

3. In same skillet, heat 2 teaspoons oil over medium-high heat until very hot; add half of beef and stir-fry until lightly browned, about 2 minutes. Transfer to bowl with broccoli mixture. Repeat with remaining 2 teaspoons oil and beef.

4. Add juice mixture to skillet, and heat to boiling; boil 1 minute. Return vegetables and beef to skillet; heat through.

Each serving: About 350 calories, 26g protein, 20g carbohydrate, 18g total fat (6g saturated), 59mg cholesterol, 525mg sodium.

Beef Stir-Fry with Arugula

We cut the prep time for this easy Asian-inspired stir-fry by using pre-sliced mushrooms and beef.

PREP: 10 MINUTES   COOK: 10 MINUTES
MAKES 4 MAIN-DISH SERVINGS.

4 teaspoons vegetable oil
1 bunch green onions, trimmed and cut into 1 1/2-inch pieces
1 package (8 ounces) sliced mushrooms
1 package (16 ounces) sliced beef for stir-fry

3 tablespoons soy sauce
3 tablespoons balsamic vinegar
2 tablespoons brown sugar
2 bunches arugula or 2 packages (8 ounces each) prewashed spinach, tough stems trimmed

1. In nonstick 12-inch skillet, heat 2 teaspoons oil over medium-high heat. Add green onions and mushrooms, and cook, stirring often, until tender and brown, about 5 minutes. Transfer to bowl.

2. In same skillet, heat 1 teaspoon oil. Add half the beef, and cook, stirring frequently (stir-frying), until beef just loses its pink color. Transfer to bowl with vegetables. Repeat with remaining beef and remaining 1 teaspoon vegetable oil.

3. In cup, mix soy sauce, balsamic vinegar, and brown sugar. Return beef mixture to skillet; stir in soy-sauce mixture. Cook, stirring, until heated through, about 1 minute. Remove from heat; stir in half the arugula.

4. Place remaining arugula on platter; top with beef mixture.

Each serving: About 260 calories, 29g protein, 18g carbohydrate, 15g total fat (5g saturated), 48mg cholesterol, 875mg sodium.

Goulash with Potato Dumplings

Old-world recipes for goulash always included some sauerkraut as we did here. Look for plastic bags of sauerkraut in the refrigerated section of the supermarket. It has a fresher taste than the canned variety.

PREP: 15 MINUTES   COOK: 15 MINUTES
MAKES 4 MAIN-DISH SERVINGS.

1 package (16 ounces) fresh or
    frozen potato dumplings (gnocchi)
2 teaspoons vegetable oil
2 garlic cloves, crushed with
    garlic press
1 medium onion, chopped
2 tablespoons paprika, preferably
    sweet Hungarian
1 tablespoon all-purpose flour

2 tablespoons tomato paste
1 cup chicken broth
1 bag (16 ounces) sauerkraut, rinsed
    and drained
1 package (17 ounces) fully cooked
    pork or beef roast au jus, cut into
    1/2-inch cubes and juices reserved
1/2 cup sour cream

1. In covered 4-quart saucepan, cook dumplings as label directs. Drain.

2. Meanwhile, in nonstick 12-inch skillet, heat oil over medium-high heat until hot. Add garlic and onion and cook, stirring occasionally, until browned, about 5 minutes. Stir in paprika and flour; cook, stirring, 1 minute. Add tomato paste; stir until blended. Add broth and heat to boiling; boil 1 minute.

3. Add sauerkraut, meat, and meat juices to skillet; heat to boiling, stirring occasionally. Reduce heat and simmer until heated through, about 1 minute. Remove skillet from heat; stir in sour cream.

4. To serve, arrange dumplings on 4 dinner plates. Spoon meat mixture over dumplings.

Each serving: About 525 calories, 35g protein, 64g carbohydrate, 16g total fat (6g saturated), 91mg cholesterol, 1,805mg sodium.

Corned Beef Hash & Eggs

Traditionally served for breakfast, this hearty skillet dish makes a wonderful Sunday night supper. It's a snap to make, too, with frozen hash brown potatoes and deli corned beef.

Prep: 5 minutes   Cook: 25 minutes
Makes 4 main-dish servings.

1 tablespoon butter or margarine
1 large red pepper, chopped
1 large onion (12 ounces), chopped
4 cups (about half 32-ounce package) frozen hash brown potatoes (Southern style)

8 ounces deli corned beef in 1 piece, cut into 1/2-inch pieces (about 2 cups)
4 large eggs
1/8 teaspoon salt
1/8 teaspoon ground black pepper

1. In nonstick 12-inch skillet, melt butter over medium-high heat. Add red pepper and onion, and cook, stirring frequently, until the vegetables are tender, about 10 minutes. Stir in frozen hash browns and corned beef; cook until hash browns are lightly browned, about 10 minutes. Spread hash evenly in skillet. Reduce heat to medium-low.

2. Break 1 egg into small cup, and, holding cup close to skillet, slip the egg into skillet; repeat with remaining eggs. Sprinkle eggs with salt and pepper. Cover skillet and cook until eggs are set or cooked to desired doneness, 5 to 8 minutes.

Each serving: About 450 calories, 22g protein, 47g carbohydrate, 20g total fat (7g saturated), 276mg cholesterol, 856mg sodium.

Corned Beef Hash and Eggs

No-Bake Tamale Pie

No-Bake Tamale Pie

Making tamale pie usually takes a bit of time and effort. But our speedy filling cooks in a skillet, and sliced precooked polenta replaces the typical saucepan topping.

PREP: 10 MINUTES   COOK: 25 MINUTES
MAKES 4 MAIN-DISH SERVINGS.

4 teaspoons vegetable oil
1 small onion, chopped
2 garlic cloves, crushed with garlic press
1 pound lean (90%) ground beef
2 teaspoons chili powder
1 teaspoon ground cumin

1/2 teaspoon salt
1 log (16 ounces) precooked polenta, cut crosswise into 8 slices
1 jar (16 ounces) medium-hot salsa
1 cup frozen whole-kernel corn
1/2 cup loosely packed fresh cilantro leaves, chopped

1. In nonstick 12-inch skillet, heat 2 teaspoons oil over medium-high heat. Add onion and cook until golden, about 3 minutes. Stir in garlic; cook 30 seconds.

2. Stir in ground beef and cook, breaking up meat with side of spoon, until meat is no longer pink, about 5 minutes. Add chili powder, cumin, and salt; cook 1 minute.

3. In nonstick 10-inch skillet, heat remaining 2 teaspoons oil over medium-high heat. Add polenta slices, and cook until golden on both sides and heated through, about 10 minutes.

4. Meanwhile, add salsa and frozen corn to meat mixture; cook 3 to 5 minutes. Stir in cilantro.

5. Spoon meat mixture into deep-dish pie plate or shallow 1 1/2-quart casserole. Arrange polenta on top.

Each serving: About 425 calories, 32g protein, 38g carbohydrate, 17g total fat (5g saturated), 69mg cholesterol, 1,325mg sodium.

Speedy Midwest Chili with Rice

If you're a fan of Cincinnati chili—that zesty beef concoction spiked with ground red pepper and cinnamon—this dish is for you.

PREP: 15 MINUTES   COOK: 15 MINUTES
MAKES 4 MAIN-DISH SERVINGS.

1 cup regular long-grain white rice
1 tablespoon vegetable oil
1 large onion (12 ounces), chopped
1 garlic clove, crushed with
   garlic press
1 pound lean (90%) ground beef
2 teaspoons chili powder
1/2 teaspoon ground cumin
1/2 teaspoon ground cinnamon

1/4 teaspoon salt
1/8 teaspoon ground red pepper
   (cayenne)
1 can (14 1/2 ounces) diced tomatoes
   in sauce
1 cup chicken broth
1 cup frozen lima beans
1/2 cup shredded Cheddar cheese

1. Cook rice as label directs.

2. Meanwhile, in nonstick 12-inch skillet, heat oil over medium-high heat. Reserve 1/4 cup chopped onion; add remaining onion to skillet, and cook until golden; about 3 minutes. Stir in garlic; cook 30 seconds.

3. Stir in ground beef, and cook, breaking up meat with side of spoon, until meat is no longer pink; about 5 minutes. Add chili powder, cumin, cinnamon, salt, and ground red pepper; cook, stirring, 30 seconds.

4. Add tomatoes and broth; heat to boiling. Reduce heat to low; simmer 5 minutes. While meat is simmering, cook lima beans as label directs.

5. To serve, spoon rice and meat mixture into 4 bowls. Sprinkle with Cheddar, lima beans, and chopped onion.

Each serving: About 620 calories, 40g protein, 57g carbohydrate, 25g total fat (11g saturated), 99mg cholesterol, 965mg sodium.

Spicy Beef with Couscous

This curry is on the milder side, so it's great for the whole family. Raisins are added to the couscous for a sweet accent.

PREP: 15 MINUTES   COOK: 15 MINUTES
MAKES 4 MAIN-DISH SERVINGS.

1 tablespoon vegetable oil
1 medium onion, chopped
2 garlic cloves, crushed with garlic press
1 teaspoon minced, peeled fresh ginger
1 pound lean (90%) ground beef
1 tablespoon curry powder
1 teaspoon garam masala spice mix
1/2 teaspoon salt

1 small yellow summer squash (about 6 ounces), cut into 1/2-inch pieces
1 cup chicken broth
1 cup frozen peas
1/2 cup loosely packed fresh cilantro leaves, chopped
1 cup plain couscous (Moroccan pasta)
1/3 cup golden raisins

1. In nonstick 12-inch skillet, heat oil over medium-high heat. Add onion and cook until golden, about 3 minutes. Stir in garlic and ginger; cook 1 minute.

2. Stir in ground beef, and cook, breaking up meat with side of spoon, until meat is no longer pink, about 5 minutes. Stir in curry, garam masala, and salt; cook 30 seconds. Add squash and cook 2 minutes.

3. Add broth and frozen peas; cook until slightly thickened. Stir in cilantro leaves.

4. Meanwhile, prepare couscous as label directs, but add raisins with the water.

5. Fluff couscous with fork and serve with beef mixture.

Each serving: About 520 calories, 34g protein, 57g carbohydrate, 16g total fat (5g saturated), 69mg cholesterol, 650mg sodium.

Mini Meatloaves in Tomato Sauce

Shape juicy ground veal into patties with Parmesan and garlic, then simmer in tomato sauce. If ground veal is difficult to find, use ground turkey instead.

PREP: 15 MINUTES   COOK: 20 MINUTES
MAKES 4 MAIN-DISH SERVINGS.

2 slices firm white bread
1/4 cup milk
1 pound ground veal or ground turkey
2 tablespoons grated Parmesan
   cheese
1/2 teaspoon salt
1/4 teaspoon coarsely ground
   black pepper

1 large egg
4 garlic cloves, minced
2 teaspoons olive oil
1 can (14 1/2 ounces) diced tomatoes
1 package (10 ounces) frozen peas
3 tablespoons heavy or whipping
   cream
1/4 cup chopped fresh basil leaves

1. In medium bowl, soak bread in milk 5 minutes; mash with fork. Stir in veal, Parmesan, salt, pepper, egg, and half of minced garlic until well blended. With hands, shape veal mixture into eight 1/2-inch-thick patties.
2. In nonstick 12-inch skillet, heat oil over medium–high heat until hot. Add patties and cook until browned, about 2 minutes per side. Reduce heat to medium. Add remaining minced garlic to skillet, and cook 1 minute. Add tomatoes with their juice and the frozen peas; cover and cook until patties are cooked through, about 10 minutes. Gently stir in cream and cook, uncovered, 2 minutes. Sprinkle with basil to serve.

Each serving: About 375 calories, 31g protein, 23g carbohydrate, 18g total fat (8g saturated), 166mg cholesterol, 895mg sodium.

Mini Meatloaves in Tomato Sauce

Sloppy José Wraps

Try making these Southwestern Sloppy Joes the next time you want to make a dinner the whole family will love.

PREP: 30 MINUTES   COOK: 40 MINUTES
MAKES 6 MAIN-DISH SERVINGS.

1 tablespoon olive oil
2 medium celery stalks, cut into
  1/4-inch pieces
1 large onion (12 ounces), cut into
  1/4-inch pieces
2 garlic cloves, crushed with
  garlic press
2 tablespoons chili powder

1 tablespoon brown sugar
1/2 teaspoon salt
1 pound lean (90%) ground beef
1 can (28 ounces) tomatoes in puree
6 (10-inch) flour tortillas, warmed
6 cups thinly sliced iceberg lettuce
  (1/2 small head)

1. In nonstick 12-inch skillet, heat oil over medium heat until hot. Add celery and onion, and cook, stirring occasionally, until vegetables are tender, about 15 minutes. Stir in garlic, chili powder, brown sugar, and salt; cook, stirring often, 2 minutes longer.

2. Increase heat to medium-high. Stir in ground beef, breaking up meat with side of spoon, and cook, stirring occasionally, until browned, 8 to 10 minutes. Add tomatoes with their puree, breaking up tomatoes with side of spoon, and cook, uncovered, stirring occasionally, until mixture thickens slightly, about 10 minutes.

3. To serve, spoon about 3/4 cup beef mixture into center of 1 warmed tortilla; top with about 1 cup lettuce and roll tortilla up. Repeat to make 5 more wraps.

Each serving: About 520 calories, 23g protein, 54g carbohydrate, 24g total fat (8g saturated), 57mg cholesterol, 1,080mg sodium.

Picadillo

Serve this intriguingly seasoned ground beef stew with a bowl of rice and a crisp green salad. If you like, cook the picadillo a little longer, until almost all the liquid has evaporated, and use it as a filling for empanadas or turnovers.

PREP: 20 MINUTES   COOK: 12 MINUTES
MAKES 4 MAIN-DISH SERVINGS.

2 teaspoons olive oil
1 medium onion, chopped
3 garlic cloves, crushed with
   garlic press
1 tablespoon chili powder
1/4 teaspoon salt
1/8 teaspoon ground cinnamon
1 pound lean (90%) ground beef

1 cup frozen whole-kernel corn
1/3 cup chopped pimiento-stuffed
   olives (salad olives)
1/4 cup dark raisins
2 tablespoons tomato paste
1/3 cup water
8 (6-inch) corn tortillas, warmed

1. In nonstick 12-inch skillet, heat oil over medium heat. Add onion and garlic and cook 5 minutes. Stir in chili powder, salt, and cinnamon; cook, stirring, 30 seconds.

2. Stir in ground beef; cook over medium-high heat, breaking up meat with side of spoon, until meat is browned, about 5 minutes. Add corn, olives, raisins, tomato paste, and water; heat to boiling. Boil until thickened slightly, about 1 minute. Serve with tortillas.

Each serving: About 465 calories, 29g protein, 47g carbohydrate, 19g total fat (6g saturated), 71mg cholesterol, 705mg sodium.

Orange-Ginger Pork Medallions

Orange-Ginger Pork Medallions

Fresh ginger is worth seeking out for its wonderful flavor. Serve the pork alongside fluffy rice topped with grated orange peel.

PREP: 10 MINUTES   COOK: 10 MINUTES
MAKES 4 MAIN-DISH SERVINGS.

1 pork tenderloin (about 1 pound)
2 medium oranges
3 teaspoons vegetable oil
1/4 teaspoon salt

1 tablespoon grated, peeled
    fresh ginger
3 green onions, trimmed and sliced

1. Cut pork tenderloin crosswise into 3/4-inch-thick pieces. With meat mallet or rolling pin, pound each piece to 1/2-inch thickness.
2. From 1 orange, grate peel and squeeze 1/2 cup juice. Cut remaining orange into 1/2-inch-thick slices; cut each slice in half. Set aside.
3. In nonstick 12-inch skillet, heat 2 teaspoons oil over medium-high heat. Add pork medallions; sprinkle with salt. Cook until pork just loses its pink color throughout, 2 to 3 minutes per side. Transfer pork to plate.
4. To same skillet, add remaining 1 teaspoon oil, and heat until hot. Add ginger, green onions, and grated orange peel, and cook until green onions are lightly browned and tender, 2 to 3 minutes. Add orange slices and juice to skillet; cook 1 minute. Return pork medallions to skillet; heat through.

Each serving: About 220 calories, 26g protein, 9g carbohydrate, 8g total fat (2g saturated), 60mg cholesterol, 215mg sodium.

Pork, Cabbage & Apple Sauté

A splash of cider vinegar adds tang to this hearty skillet supper of pan-browned pork chops, shredded cabbage, sliced apples, red potatoes, and caramelized onions.

PREP: 15 MINUTES   COOK: 40 MINUTES
MAKES 4 MAIN-DISH SERVINGS.

1 teaspoon olive oil
4 bone-in pork loin chops, 3/4 inch
    thick (about 6 ounces each),
    trimmed
3/4 teaspoon salt
1/4 teaspoon ground black pepper
1 large onion (12 ounces),
    thinly sliced
1 bag (16 ounces) shredded cabbage
    mix for coleslaw

2 large Golden Delicious or Gala
    apples (about 8 ounces each),
    cored and cut into 1/2-inch-thick
    slices
12 ounces red potatoes, cut into
    1-inch pieces
3/4 cup apple cider
1/4 teaspoon dried thyme
1 tablespoon cider vinegar

1. In nonstick 12-inch skillet, heat oil over medium-high heat until very hot. Add pork chops; sprinkle with 1/4 teaspoon salt and 1/8 teaspoon pepper. Cook chops until golden on the outside and still slightly pink on the inside, about 4 minutes per side. Transfer the chops to a plate; keep warm.
2. Add onion to skillet, and cook over medium heat, covered, stirring occasionally, until tender and golden, 8 to 10 minutes. Gradually stir in the cabbage mix and cook until wilted, about 5 minutes. Add apples, potatoes, apple cider, thyme, and remaining 1/2 teaspoon salt and 1/8 teaspoon pepper; heat to boiling. Reduce heat to medium-low, and simmer, covered, until potatoes are tender, about 15 minutes.
3. Stir in vinegar. Tuck chops into cabbage mixture and heat through.

Each serving: About 380 calories, 26g protein, 46g carbohydrate, 11g total fat (3g saturated), 69mg cholesterol, 535mg sodium.

Pork, Cabbage & Apple Sauté

Brazilian Pork

Brazilian Pork

This tasty dish is an excellent example of Brazilian cuisine: spicy, with a hint of citrus and accompanied by black beans.

PREP: 15 MINUTES   COOK: 15 MINUTES
MAKES 4 MAIN-DISH SERVINGS.

4 boneless pork loin chops,
   3/4 inch thick (5 ounces each),
   trimmed
1/2 teaspoon ground cumin
1/2 teaspoon ground coriander
1/4 teaspoon dried thyme
1/8 teaspoon ground allspice
1/2 teaspoon salt
1 teaspoon olive oil
1 medium onion, chopped
3 garlic cloves, crushed with
   garlic press

1 can (15 to 19 ounces) black beans,
   rinsed and drained
1/2 cup chicken broth
1 tablespoon fresh lime juice
1/4 teaspoon coarsely ground
   black pepper
1/4 cup packed fresh cilantro leaves,
   chopped
fresh orange wedges (optional)

1. Pat pork chops dry with paper towels. In cup, mix cumin, coriander, thyme, allspice, and 1/4 teaspoon salt. Rub pork chops with spice mixture.
2. Heat nonstick 12-inch skillet over medium-high heat until hot. Add pork chops and cook, until lightly browned on the outside and still slightly pink on the inside, about 4 minutes per side. Transfer pork to platter; keep warm.
3. In same skillet, heat olive oil over medium heat. Add onion and cook, stirring frequently, until golden, about 5 minutes. Add the garlic and cook, stirring, 1 minute longer. Add beans, chicken broth, lime juice, pepper, and remaining 1/4 teaspoon salt; heat through.
4. To serve, spoon bean mixture over pork; sprinkle with cilantro. Serve with orange wedges, if you like.

Each serving: About 340 calories, 42g protein, 25g carbohydrate, 11g total fat (3g saturated), 76mg cholesterol, 760mg sodium.

Applesauce Pork

Make this dish on a cool autumn evening, when apples are at their flavorful best. We like the chops served over a bed of couscous or egg noodles.

Prep: 10 minutes   Cook: 20 minutes
Makes 4 main-dish servings.

4 boneless pork loin chops,
  3/4 inch thick (5 ounces each),
  trimmed
1/2 teaspoon salt
1/4 teaspoon coarsely ground black
  pepper
1 tablespoon butter or margarine

2 large Golden Delicious apples
  (about 1 pound), peeled, cored, and
  each cut into 12 wedges
1 medium onion, chopped
1/2 cup pitted prunes, chopped
3/4 cup apple juice
1 tablespoon cider vinegar

1. Pat pork chops dry with paper towels. Sprinkle pork chops with 1/4 teaspoon salt and pepper.

2. Heat nonstick 12-inch skillet over medium-high heat until hot. Add pork chops and cook until lightly browned on the outside and still slightly pink on the inside, about 4 minutes per side. Transfer pork to platter; keep warm.

3. In same skillet, melt butter over medium heat. Add apples, onion, prunes, and remaining 1/4 teaspoon salt. Cook, covered, until apples and onion are tender and golden, about 10 minutes, stirring occasionally.

4. Remove cover. Add apple juice and vinegar; heat to boiling.

5. To serve, spoon apple mixture over pork chops.

Each serving: About 365 calories, 32g protein, 33g carbohydrate, 12g total fat (5g saturated), 86mg cholesterol, 381mg sodium.

Applesauce Pork

Pork Chops with Peppers & Onions

Boneless chops are smothered in green onions and red peppers for this fast and easy skillet dinner.

PREP: 10 MINUTES   COOK: 20 MINUTES
MAKES 4 MAIN-DISH SERVINGS.

4 boneless pork loin chops, 1/2 inch thick (about 4 ounces each), trimmed
1/2 teaspoon salt
1/4 teaspoon ground black pepper
2 teaspoons olive oil
1 bunch green onions, green tops cut diagonally into 3-inch pieces and white bottoms thinly sliced crosswise

2 medium red peppers, cut into 1 1/2-inch pieces
1 garlic clove, crushed with garlic press
1/8 teaspoon crushed red pepper
1/2 cup chicken broth

1. Heat nonstick 12-inch skillet over medium-high heat until hot but not smoking. Add pork chops to skillet and sprinkle with salt and pepper. Cook chops until lightly browned on the outside and still slightly pink on the inside, about 4 minutes per side (reduce heat to medium if chops are browning too quickly). Transfer chops to plate; keep warm.

2. To same skillet, add oil and green-onion tops; cook 4 minutes. With slotted spoon, transfer green-onion tops to small bowl.

3. In same skillet, cook red peppers and green-onion bottoms, stirring occasionally, 8 minutes. Add garlic and crushed red pepper, and cook, stirring, 1 minute. Stir in broth and half of green-onion tops; heat through.

4. To serve, spoon pepper mixture onto platter; top with chops and the remaining green-onion tops.

Each serving: About 210 calories, 26g protein, 7g carbohydrate, 8g total fat (2g saturated), 71mg cholesterol, 495mg sodium.

Pork Chops with Peppers & Onions

Boneless BBQ "Ribs"

All the great flavors of a summertime barbecue—without the work of heating up a grill. Serve with your favorite beans, which can heat while the pork cooks, and—if you have time—a crisp salad.

PREP: 10 MINUTES   COOK: 7 MINUTES
MAKES 4 MAIN-DISH SERVINGS.

3 tablespoons chili sauce
1 tablespoon mild molasses
2 teaspoons brown sugar
2 teaspoons minced, peeled
  fresh ginger
2 teaspoons Worcestershire sauce

2 teaspoons cider vinegar
1 teaspoon cornstarch
1/8 teaspoon salt
1 tablespoon water
1 pound boneless pork "ribs"
  (see Tip below)

1. In small bowl, with fork, stir chili sauce, molasses, brown sugar, ginger, Worcestershire, vinegar, cornstarch, salt, and water; set aside.

2. Heat nonstick 12-inch skillet over medium-high heat until hot. Add pork ribs and cook until they are lightly browned on the outside and just lose their pink color on the inside, about 2 to 3 minutes per side.

3. Reduce heat to low; add sauce to pork, and cook until sauce bubbles and thickens, 30 seconds to 1 minute.

Each serving: About 205 calories, 25g protein, 10g carbohydrate, 7g total fat (2g saturated), 58mg cholesterol, 290mg sodium.

Tip

If you can't find boneless pork ribs at the market, follow our easy instructions (at right) for cutting a 1-pound boneless pork loin roast into "ribs."

A. Holding sharp chef's knife parallel to work surface, cut a well-trimmed 1-pound boneless pork loin roast horizontally in half.

B. Cut each half crosswise into 8 strips (or 10 strips if thinner "ribs" are desired).

Orange Pork & Asparagus Stir-Fry

Slices of lean pork tenderloin are quickly cooked with fresh asparagus and juicy orange pieces.

PREP: 20 MINUTES   COOK: 6 MINUTES
MAKES 4 MAIN-DISH SERVINGS.

2 navel oranges
1 teaspoon olive oil
1 whole pork tenderloin (about 3/4 pound), trimmed and thinly sliced diagonally
3/4 teaspoon salt
1/4 teaspoon ground black pepper

1 1/2 pounds thin asparagus, trimmed and each stalk cut crosswise in half
1 garlic clove, crushed with garlic press
1/4 cup water

1. From 1 orange, grate 1 teaspoon peel and squeeze 1/4 cup juice. Remove peel and white pith from remaining orange. Cut orange into 1/4-inch-thick slices; cut each slice into quarters.

2. In nonstick 12-inch skillet, heat 1/2 teaspoon oil over medium-high heat until hot but not smoking. Add half the pork, and sprinkle with 1/4 teaspoon salt and 1/8 teaspoon pepper; cook, stirring frequently (stir-frying), until pork just loses its pink color, 2 minutes. Transfer pork to plate. Repeat with remaining 1/2 teaspoon oil, pork, 1/4 teaspoon salt, and remaining 1/8 teaspoon pepper. Transfer pork to same plate.

3. To the same skillet, add asparagus, garlic, grated orange peel, remaining 1/4 teaspoon salt, and water; cover and cook, stirring occasionally, until asparagus is tender-crisp, about 2 minutes. Return pork to skillet. Add orange juice and orange pieces; heat through, stirring often.

Each serving: About 165 calories, 24g protein, 8g carbohydrate, 4g total fat (1g saturated), 50mg cholesterol, 495mg sodium.

Orange Pork & Asparagus Stir-Fry

Asian Pork & Baby Peas

Asian Pork & Baby Peas

Pair with an aromatic grain such as basmati rice. Cucumber salad makes a nice accompaniment.

PREP: 10 MINUTES   COOK: 10 MINUTES
MAKES 4 MAIN-DISH SERVINGS.

2 teaspoons vegetable oil
1 pork tenderloin (about 1 pound), cut into 1/4-inch-thick slices
2 garlic cloves, crushed with garlic press
1 package (10 ounces) frozen baby peas

3 tablespoons reduced-sodium soy sauce
2 tablespoons seasoned rice vinegar
1 tablespoon grated, peeled fresh ginger
1 tablespoon mild molasses
1/4 teaspoon crushed red pepper

1. In nonstick 12-inch skillet, heat oil over medium–high heat until hot. Add pork slices and garlic, and cook, stirring occasionally, until pork is browned on the outside and just loses its pink color on the inside, about 6 minutes. Transfer pork to plate; keep warm

2. To same skillet, add frozen peas, soy sauce, rice vinegar, ginger, molasses, and crushed red pepper; cook until peas are heated through, about 4 minutes. Return pork to skillet; toss to coat.

Each serving: About 230 calories, 28g protein, 19g carbohydrate, 6g total fat (1g saturated), 64mg cholesterol, 840mg sodium.

Pork Chops with Apples & Cream

To bring out the flavor of the apples, we spiked this dish with Calvados, an apple brandy made in the Normandy region of northern France. Less-expensive applejack is a good substitute.

PREP: 10 MINUTES   COOK: 1 HOUR TO 1 HOUR 15 MINUTES
MAKES 4 MAIN-DISH SERVINGS.

4 pork loin chops, each 3/4 inch thick
  (about 6 ounces each)
1/2 teaspoon salt
1/4 teaspoon ground black pepper
2 teaspoons vegetable oil
1 small onion, finely chopped
1/4 cup Calvados or applejack brandy

1 cup chicken broth
1/8 teaspoon dried thyme
3 medium Golden Delicious apples,
  peeled, cored, and each cut
  into quarters
1/2 cup heavy or whipping cream

1. Pat pork chops dry with paper towels. Sprinkle with salt and pepper.

2. In 12-inch skillet, heat oil over medium-high heat. Add pork chops and cook until lightly browned on both sides. Transfer chops to plate as they brown; keep warm.

3. To drippings in skillet, add onion and cook over medium heat until tender, about 3 minutes. Add Calvados and cook until the liquid has almost evaporated.

4. Return chops to skillet; add broth, thyme, and apples; heat to boiling over high heat. Reduce heat to low; cover skillet and simmer until chops are tender, 30 to 45 minutes.

5. Transfer chops and apples to warm platter; keep warm. Increase heat to high; boil liquid in skillet, uncovered, until reduced to 1/2 cup, about 5 minutes. Add cream; heat to boiling. Boil 3 minutes.

6. To serve, spoon cream sauce over pork chops.

Each serving: About 485 calories, 31g protein, 23g carbohydrate, 27g total fat (12g saturated), 110mg cholesterol, 610mg sodium.

Dan-Dan Noodles

We made this popular Chinese noodle dish, a specialty of the Szechuan province, with easy-to-find fresh fettuccine, available in the supermarket dairy case, in place of *sun mian*, a Chinese wheat noodle.

PREP: 20 MINUTES   COOK: 20 MINUTES
MAKES 4 MAIN-DISH SERVINGS.

1/2 cup chicken broth
1/4 cup soy sauce
2 tablespoons sugar
1 tablespoon creamy peanut butter
2 teaspoons cornstarch
2 teaspoons Asian sesame oil
1/4 teaspoon crushed red pepper
8 ounces ground pork
1 tablespoon grated, peeled
    fresh ginger

2 garlic cloves, crushed with
    garlic press
3 green onions, thinly sliced
1 small head (12 ounces) napa
    (Chinese) cabbage, trimmed
    and sliced (about 4 cups)
salt
1 package (9 ounces) fresh
    fettuccine

1. In small bowl, with wire whisk or fork, mix broth, soy sauce, sugar, peanut butter, cornstarch, oil, and crushed red pepper; set aside.

2. Heat nonstick 12-inch skillet over medium-high heat until very hot. Add pork, ginger, garlic, and green onions, and cook, breaking up pork with side of spoon and stirring occasionally, until pork is browned, 6 to 8 minutes. Transfer pork mixture to small bowl.

3. In same skillet, cook cabbage, stirring frequently, until lightly browned, about 5 minutes.

4. Meanwhile, in large saucepot, cook fettuccine as label directs.

5. Return pork mixture to skillet. Stir in broth mixture; heat to boiling. Reduce heat to medium, and simmer, uncovered, until sauce has thickened slightly, about 2 minutes.

6. To serve, drain fettuccine; toss with pork mixture in skillet.

Each serving: About 420 calories, 21g protein, 48g carbohydrate, 16g total fat (5g saturated), 106mg cholesterol, 1,315mg sodium.

Middle Eastern Lamb Steaks

Middle Eastern Lamb Steaks

Aromatic spices such as coriander, cumin, and allspice in a quick tomato relish add zip to simple pan-seared lamb steaks.

PREP: ABOUT 15 MINUTES   COOK: 20 MINUTES
MAKES 4 MAIN-DISH SERVINGS.

1 teaspoon dried thyme
1 teaspoon ground coriander
1 teaspoon ground cumin
1/2 teaspoon ground allspice
1/2 teaspoon salt
1/4 teaspoon ground black pepper
1 can (28 ounces) whole tomatoes
1 teaspoon vegetable oil

1 medium red onion, chopped
1/4 cup dried currants
1 tablespoon pine nuts (optional)
2 tablespoons chopped fresh parsley
  leaves
2 center-cut lamb leg steaks, each
  3/4 inch thick (about 8 ounces
  each), trimmed

1. In small bowl, with fork, stir thyme, coriander, cumin, allspice, salt, and pepper. Drain tomatoes, reserving 1/2 cup juice; chop tomatoes.

2. In nonstick 12-inch skillet, heat oil over medium heat until hot. Add onion and 2 teaspoons thyme mixture, and cook, stirring occasionally, until onion is slightly softened, about 5 minutes. Add chopped tomatoes, reserved juice, and currants, and cook, stirring occasionally, until slightly thickened, about 6 minutes. Transfer tomato mixture to bowl; stir in pine nuts, if using, and 1 tablespoon parsley.

3. Coat lamb steaks with remaining thyme mixture. In same skillet, cook lamb over medium-high heat 4 to 5 minutes per side for medium-rare, or until desired doneness.

4. To serve, spoon tomato relish into deep platter; top with lamb and sprinkle with remaining 1 tablespoon parsley.

Each serving: About 255 calories, 26g protein, 17g carbohydrate, 9g total fat (3g saturated), 78mg cholesterol, 555mg sodium.

Mafalda with Lamb & Mint

A savory Moroccan-inspired mixture of spices adds bold flavor to this comforting pasta dish, which uses long ruffle-edged noodles.

PREP: 15 MINUTES   COOK: 25 MINUTES
MAKES 6 MAIN-DISH SERVINGS.

12 ounces mafalda noodles or
  fettuccine
1 tablespoon olive oil
1 large onion (12 ounces), cut into
  1/4-inch pieces
1 medium red pepper, cut into
  1/4-inch pieces
12 ounces ground lamb
3 garlic cloves, minced
2 teaspoons dried mint

2 teaspoons ground coriander
3/4 teaspoon salt
1/2 teaspoon ground red pepper
  (cayenne)
1 can (28 ounces) whole tomatoes
  in juice
3 tablespoons tomato paste
1/2 cup loosely packed fresh parsley
  leaves, chopped

1. In large saucepot, cook *mafalda* as label directs.

2. Meanwhile, in nonstick 12-inch skillet, heat oil over medium heat until hot. Add onion and red pepper, and cook, stirring occasionally, until lightly browned and almost tender, about 10 minutes. Increase heat to medium-high; add lamb, garlic, mint, coriander, salt, and ground red pepper, and cook, stirring occasionally, until browned, about 8 minutes.

3. Stir in tomatoes with their juice and tomato paste, breaking up tomatoes with side of spoon; heat to boiling. Reduce heat to medium and simmer, uncovered, 5 minutes.

4. Drain *mafalda*; return to saucepot. Add lamb mixture and chopped parsley; toss to coat.

Each serving: About 440 calories, 19g protein, 55g carbohydrate, 17g total fat (6g saturated), 41mg cholesterol, 780mg sodium.

New Orleans-Style Rice & Beans

Our easy take on this classic Southern recipe is as hearty and satisfying as its longer-cooking cousin. Enjoy with your favorite hot pepper sauce.

PREP: 5 MINUTES   COOK: 20 MINUTES
MAKES 4 MAIN-DISH SERVINGS.

1 1/3 cups regular long-grain
   white rice
1 tablespoon olive oil
1 large onion (12 ounces), chopped
1 medium stalk celery, trimmed
   and sliced
3 garlic cloves, finely chopped
1 can (15 to 19 ounces) low-sodium
   red kidney beans

1 can (15 to 19 ounces) low-sodium
   pink beans
1 reduced-sodium ham steak, 1/2 inch
   thick (about 1 1/4 pounds), cut into
   1/2-inch cubes
1/2 teaspoon dried thyme
1/4 teaspoon ground black pepper

1. Cook rice as label directs.
2. Meanwhile, in nonstick 12-inch skillet, heat oil over medium heat until hot. Add onion, celery, and garlic, and cook, stirring occasionally, until vegetables are tender and lightly browned, 7 to 8 minutes.
3. Stir in beans with their liquid, ham, thyme, and pepper; heat to boiling over medium-high heat. Reduce heat to low; simmer until mixture thickens slightly, about 10 minutes.
4. To serve, spoon rice into deep platter; top with bean mixture.

Each serving: About 670 calories, 42g protein, 103g carbohydrate, 10g total fat (3g saturated), 68mg cholesterol, 1,185mg sodium.

SEAFOOD

Paella Pronto
recipe on page 145

Sherried Flounder

Sherry adds balance to the creamy clam chowder and doesn't overpower the flounder's mild flavor. Steamed green beans and hot white rice are perfect accompaniments.

PREP: 5 MINUTES COOK: 15 MINUTES
MAKES 4 MAIN-DISH SERVINGS.

1 bunch green onions, trimmed
2 teaspoons olive oil
1 large red pepper, thinly sliced
1/4 cup dry sherry
1 can (15 to 18.5 ounces) ready-to-
 serve clam chowder

1/8 teaspoon ground black pepper
4 flounder fillets (about
 6 ounces each)

1. Thinly slice 1 green onion; reserve for garnish. Cut remaining green onions into 2-inch pieces.

2. In nonstick 12-inch skillet, heat oil over medium-high heat until hot. Add green-onion pieces and red pepper, and cook, stirring occasionally, until pepper is tender-crisp, about 5 minutes.

3. Add sherry to skillet and cook until liquid is reduced by half, about 30 seconds. Stir in clam chowder and black pepper; heat to boiling, stirring frequently.

4. Reduce heat to medium. Place flounder on top of soup mixture; cover and cook, until just opaque throughout, 3 to 4 minutes.

5. With metal spatula, carefully transfer flounder to platter. Spoon soup mixture over flounder. Sprinkle with reserved sliced green onion.

Each serving: About 340 calories, 37g protein, 18g carbohydrate, 13g total fat (4g saturated), 87mg cholesterol, 695mg sodium.

Cod with Peppers & Onions

Serve this with bagged salad greens tossed with a sliced pear (leave the skin on) and your favorite balsamic vinaigrette.

PREP: 15 MINUTES   COOK: 20 MINUTES
MAKES 2 MAIN-DISH SERVINGS.

1 1/2 cups small shell pasta (about 6 ounces)
1 tablespoon olive oil
1 small onion, thinly sliced
1/2 small red pepper, thinly sliced
1/2 small yellow pepper, thinly sliced
1 garlic clove, finely chopped
1/4 teaspoon fennel seeds, crushed (optional)

1 can (14 1/2 ounces) diced tomatoes in juice
2 cod fillets or other mild white fish, 3/4 inch thick (about 6 ounces each)
1/4 teaspoon salt
pinch coarsely ground black pepper

1. In large saucepot, cook pasta as label directs.

2. Meanwhile, in nonstick 12-inch skillet, heat oil over medium-high heat until hot. Add onion, red and yellow peppers, garlic, and fennel seeds (if using); cook, stirring the mixture frequently, until vegetables are tender, about 5 minutes.

3. Stir in tomatoes with their juice; heat to boiling. Reduce heat to low and simmer 5 minutes.

4. Place cod fillets on top of tomato mixture in skillet. Sprinkle cod with 1/4 teaspoon salt and pepper. Cover skillet and simmer, occasionally spooning sauce over cod, until cod flakes easily when tested with a fork and turns opaque throughout, 8 to 10 minutes.

5. To serve, drain pasta; spoon into 2 bowls. Top with cod and sauce.

Each serving: About 580 calories, 44g protein, 78g carbohydrate, 10g total fat (1g saturated), 73mg cholesterol, 1,200mg sodium.

Latin-Style Fish with Black Beans

Latin-Style Fish with Black Beans

Rich fish, such as Chilean sea bass or salmon, or lean, meaty fish like halibut tastes great with this zesty black-bean mixture. Best of all, you only need one skillet.

Prep: 20 minutes   Cook: 30 minutes
Makes 4 main-dish servings.

FISH
1 tablespoon vegetable oil
4 Chilean sea bass or salmon fillets
  (about 6 ounces each)
1 teaspoon freshly grated
  orange peel
1/4 teaspoon salt
1/4 teaspoon dried oregano

BLACK BEANS
1 small onion, cut into 1/4-inch pieces
2 garlic cloves, crushed with
  garlic press

1 small jalapeño chile, seeded
  and minced
1/4 teaspoon dried oregano
2 green onions, trimmed and chopped
1 can (15 to 19 ounces) black beans,
  rinsed and drained
1/3 cup fresh orange juice
2 tablespoons fresh lime juice
1 cup loosely packed fresh cilantro
  leaves, chopped

1. Prepare Fish: In nonstick 12-inch skillet, heat oil over medium–high heat until hot. Rub fish fillets with orange peel, salt, and oregano. Add fish to skillet, and cook until golden brown on the outside and opaque throughout, 4 to 7 minutes per side (depending on thickness). Transfer fish to platter; keep warm. Pour drippings in skillet into small bowl; reserve. Wipe skillet with paper towel.

2. Prepare Black Beans: In same skillet, heat 1 tablespoon reserved drippings over medium heat. Add onion, garlic, jalapeño, and oregano, and cook, stirring occasionally, until onion is tender and golden, about 10 minutes. Add green onions and cook, stirring occasionally, 2 minutes longer. Stir in beans, orange juice, and lime juice; heat to boiling. Reduce heat to low; simmer, uncovered, until heated through, about 2 minutes.

3. To serve, pour black-bean mixture over fish, and sprinkle with cilantro.

Each serving: About 320 calories, 42g protein, 25g carbohydrate, 8g total fat (1g saturated), 54mg cholesterol, 520mg sodium.

Salmon & Asparagus Stir-Fry

For a change of pace, we cut a salmon fillet into bite-size pieces and stir-fried it with spring veggies. Serve with brown or white rice, if you like.

Prep: 25 minutes   Cook: 15 minutes
Makes 4 main-dish servings.

1 1/2 pounds skinless salmon fillet
  or swordfish steak, cut into
  1 1/2-inch pieces
1/4 teaspoon salt
1/4 teaspoon coarsely ground
  black pepper
1 1/2 pounds asparagus, trimmed and
  cut into 2-inch pieces
1 medium red pepper, thinly sliced
3 green onions, trimmed and
  thinly sliced

3 tablespoons soy sauce
2 tablespoons seasoned rice vinegar
1 tablespoon grated, peeled
  fresh ginger
1 garlic clove, crushed with
  garlic press
1 teaspoon cornstarch
1/2 teaspoon sugar
3/4 cup water

1. Heat nonstick 12-inch skillet or wok over medium-high heat until hot. Add fish, and sprinkle with salt and pepper. Cook fish, gently stirring occasionally, until fish turns opaque throughout, 5 to 7 minutes. Transfer fish to platter; keep warm.

2. To same skillet, add asparagus and red pepper, and cook, covered, until vegetables are tender-crisp, stirring occasionally, about 5 minutes.

3. Meanwhile, in small bowl, with wire whisk or fork, mix green onions, soy sauce, vinegar, ginger, garlic, cornstarch, sugar, and water until blended. Add soy-sauce mixture to the vegetables and heat to boiling. Boil 1 minute, stirring constantly. Spoon vegetable mixture over fish; toss gently before serving.

Each serving: About 265 calories, 38g protein, 11g carbohydrate, 7g total fat (1g saturated), 89mg cholesterol, 1,280mg sodium.

Salmon & Asparagus Stir-Fry

Bow Ties with Salmon & Peas

Bow Ties with Salmon & Peas

Sauté chunks of fresh salmon and toss with a lemony dill sauce for a luscious main dish that sings of spring no matter what the season.

PREP: 15 MINUTES   COOK: ABOUT 15 MINUTES
MAKES 6 MAIN-DISH SERVINGS.

1 package (16 ounces) bow-tie or
  corkscrew pasta
2 lemons
2 tablespoons butter or margarine
2 large shallots, thinly sliced
  (1/2 cup)
1 pound skinless salmon fillet, cut
  into 1-inch pieces

1 teaspoon salt
1/4 teaspoon ground black pepper
1 package (10 ounces) frozen peas
1/2 cup loosely packed fresh dill,
  chopped

1. In large saucepot cook pasta as label directs.

2. Meanwhile, from lemons, grate 2 teaspoons peel and squeeze 3 tablespoons juice; set aside.

3. In nonstick 12-inch skillet, melt butter over medium heat. Add shallots and cook, stirring occasionally, until tender-crisp, about 2 minutes. Increase heat to medium-high. Add salmon, salt, pepper, and lemon peel, and cook, gently stirring occasionally, until salmon turns opaque throughout, about 5 minutes.

4. Drain pasta, reserving *1/3 cup cooking water*; add to salmon mixture, stirring gently to combine. Place frozen peas in colander; drain pasta over peas. Return pasta and peas to saucepot. Add salmon mixture, chopped dill, and lemon juice; toss gently to combine.

Each serving: About 470 calories, 28g protein, 66g carbohydrate, 10g total fat (4g saturated), 50g cholesterol, 668mg sodium.

Scrod with Slaw & Bacon

A touch of bacon adds heartiness to this lowfat main dish of fish fillets that are steamed on top of wilted, preshredded cabbage slaw. Serve with a chunk of crusty bread to complete the meal.

PREP: 10 MINUTES   COOK: 20 MINUTES
MAKES 4 MAIN-DISH SERVINGS.

2 slices bacon
1 bag (16 ounces) shredded cabbage
    mix for coleslaw
3/4 teaspoon salt
1/4 teaspoon coarsely ground
    black pepper

4 pieces scrod fillet (about 6 ounces
    each)
1/4 cup loosely packed fresh parsley
    leaves, chopped

1. In nonstick 12-inch skillet, cook bacon over medium heat until browned. With slotted spoon, transfer bacon to paper towels to drain.
2. Increase heat to medium-high. To drippings remaining in skillet, add cabbage mix, 1/2 teaspoon salt, and pepper. Cover skillet and cook, stirring occasionally, until cabbage wilts, about 5 minutes.
3. Arrange scrod over cabbage; sprinkle with remaining 1/4 teaspoon salt. Cover and cook until fish flakes easily when tested with a fork, 6 to 8 minutes longer. Sprinkle scrod with bacon and parsley to serve.

Each serving: About 185 calories, 33g protein, 36g carbohydrate, 3g total fat (1g saturated), 76mg cholesterol, 565mg sodium.

Fisherman's Stew

Fennel and tomato accent this seafood trio of monkfish, shrimp, and mussels. Serve with crusty bread. Double this one when company's coming—just make sure to use a large Dutch oven instead of a skillet.

PREP: 30 MINUTES   COOK: 25 MINUTES
MAKES 4 MAIN-DISH SERVINGS.

2 teaspoons olive oil
1 medium onion, chopped
1 medium fennel bulb (about
   1 pound), trimmed, cored, and
   thinly sliced
1/2 teaspoon salt
1/8 teaspoon coarsely ground
   black pepper
1 large lemon
2 garlic cloves, crushed with
   garlic press
1 bottle (8 ounces) clam juice
1/2 cup dry white wine

1 can (14 1/2 ounces) diced tomatoes
1 pound monkfish, dark membrane
   and bones discarded (if any), or
   cod, cut into 1 1/2-inch pieces
1 pound mussels, scrubbed and
   beards removed
8 ounces large shrimp, shelled and
   deveined, leaving tail part of shell
   on if you like
1/2 cup loosely packed fresh parsley
   leaves, chopped

1. In deep nonstick 12-inch skillet, heat oil over medium-high heat until hot. Add onion, fennel, salt, and pepper, and cook, covered, until vegetables are tender and golden, stirring occasionally, about 10 minutes.

2. Meanwhile, from lemon, with vegetable peeler, remove 3 strips peel (3" by 3/4" each).

3. Add garlic to skillet and cook 30 seconds. Add clam juice, wine, and lemon peel; heat to boiling. Boil 1 minute. Reduce heat to medium-low and simmer, stirring occasionally, 5 minutes.

4. Stir in tomatoes with their juice; heat to boiling over medium-high heat. Add monkfish, mussels, and shrimp; heat to boiling. Reduce heat to medium-low, and simmer, covered, until fish and shrimp turn opaque throughout and mussel shells open, 6 to 7 minutes. Remove lemon peel and discard. Sprinkle with parsley just before serving.

Each serving: About 265 calories, 34g protein, 17g carbohydrate, 6g total fat (1g saturated), 111mg cholesterol, 1,145mg sodium.

Shrimp & Pea Risotto

Turn a classic risotto—traditionally served as a first course—into a lovely main course by adding shrimp and peas.

PREP: 20 MINUTES   COOK: 40 MINUTES
MAKES 4 MAIN-DISH SERVINGS.

2 tablespoons butter or margarine
12 ounces large shrimp, shelled, deveined, and cut crosswise into thirds
1 cup frozen peas
3/4 teaspoon salt
1 medium onion, finely chopped
1 can (14 1/2 ounces) vegetable broth or chicken broth

3 1/2 cups water
2 cups Carnaroli or Arborio rice (Italian short-grain rice) or regular medium-grain rice
1/4 teaspoon coarsely ground black pepper
1/2 cup dry white wine

1. In nonstick 10-inch skillet, heat 1 tablespoon butter over medium-high heat until melted. Add shrimp and cook, stirring, until shrimp turn opaque throughout, about 2 minutes. Add peas and 1/4 teaspoon salt, and cook, stirring, 1 minute; set aside.

2. In wide-bottomed 4 1/2- to 5-quart saucepot or Dutch oven, melt remaining 1 tablespoon butter over medium heat. Add onion and cook, stirring occasionally, until tender, about 10 minutes.

3. Meanwhile, in 3-quart saucepan, heat broth and water to boiling over high heat. Reduce heat to low to maintain simmer; cover.

4. Add rice, remaining 1/2 teaspoon salt, and pepper to onion in saucepot, and cook, stirring often, until rice grains turn opaque, 2 to 3 minutes. Increase heat to medium-high; add wine and cook, stirring, until wine has been absorbed. Add 1/2 cup simmering broth mixture, stirring until liquid is absorbed.

5. Continue cooking, adding remaining broth, 1/2 cup at a time, and stirring after each addition, until liquid is absorbed and rice is tender but still firm, about 20 minutes (risotto should have a creamy consistency). Stir in shrimp mixture; heat through.

Each serving: About 605 calories, 26g protein, 101g carbohydrate, 8g total fat (4g saturated), 124mg cholesterol, 1,067mg sodium.

Shrimp & Pea Risotto

Greek Shrimp & Potatoes

Greek Shrimp & Potatoes

Simple and satisfying with garlic, canned tomatoes, fresh dill, and crumbled feta—yet only 310 calories per serving.

PREP: 25 MINUTES   COOK: 40 MINUTES
MAKES 4 MAIN-DISH SERVINGS.

2 teaspoons olive oil
1 large onion (12 ounces), chopped
1 1/2 pounds all-purpose potatoes,
    peeled and cut into 1-inch pieces
1 large garlic clove, crushed with
    garlic press
1/8 teaspoon ground red pepper
    (cayenne)
1/2 teaspoon salt

1 cup water
1 can (14 1/2 ounces) diced tomatoes
1 pound large shrimp, shelled and
    deveined, leaving tail part on
    if you like
2 tablespoons chopped fresh dill
2 ounces crumbled feta cheese
    (about 1/2 cup)

1. In nonstick 10-inch skillet, heat oil over medium heat. Add onion and cook, stirring often, until tender, about 10 minutes.

2. Add potatoes, garlic, and ground red pepper, and cook 30 seconds. Stir in salt and water; heat to boiling over high heat. Reduce heat to low; cover and simmer until potatoes are tender, about 15 minutes.

3. Add tomatoes with their juice; heat to boiling over high heat. Reduce heat to low; cover and simmer 5 minutes. Remove cover; simmer for 5 minutes longer.

4. Stir in shrimp; heat to boiling over high heat. Reduce heat to low; cover and simmer, until shrimp turn opaque throughout, 3 to 5 minutes. Remove skillet from heat; stir in chopped dill and feta cheese. Spoon into bowls.

Each serving: About 310 calories, 25g protein, 36g carbohydrate, 7g total fat (3g saturated), 155mg cholesterol, 740mg sodium.

Pad Thai

A delicious mix of noodles, shrimp, peanuts, garlic, and eggs. This dish cooks quickly, so have everything in place before you start. Rice stick noodles and Asian fish sauce are available in Asian groceries.

PREP: 25 MINUTES   COOK: 5 MINUTES   MAKES 4 MAIN-DISH SERVINGS.

1 package (7 to 8 ounces) flat rice stick noodles, broken in half, or 8 ounces angel hair pasta
8 ounces medium shrimp, shelled and deveined
1/4 cup fresh lime juice
1/4 cup Asian fish sauce (nuoc nam) (see Tip page 50)
2 tablespoons sugar
1 tablespoon vegetable oil
2 garlic cloves, crushed with garlic press

1/4 teaspoon crushed red pepper
2 large eggs, lightly beaten
6 ounces fresh bean sprouts (about 2 cups), rinsed and drained
2 tablespoons unsalted roasted peanuts, coarsely chopped
3 green onions, trimmed and thinly sliced
1/2 cup loosely packed cilantro leaves
lime wedges

1. In large bowl, soak rice stick noodles in hot tap water to cover 20 minutes. (Or, break angel hair pasta in half; cook as label directs, and rinse under cold running water.)

2. Meanwhile, cut each shrimp horizontally in half. In small bowl, combine lime juice, fish sauce, and sugar. Assemble all remaining ingredients before beginning to cook.

3. Drain noodles. In nonstick wok or 12-inch skillet, heat oil over high heat until hot but not smoking. Add shrimp, garlic, and crushed red pepper, and cook, stirring frequently (stir-frying), 1 minute. Add eggs and cook, stir-frying, 2 minutes. Add lime-juice mixture, half of bean sprouts, half of peanuts, and half of green onions; cook, stir-frying, 1 minute.

4. Transfer noodle mixture to platter; top with remaining bean sprouts, peanuts, and green onions. Sprinkle with cilantro. Serve with lime wedges.

Each serving: About 395 calories, 19g protein, 59g carbohydrate, 9g total fat (2g saturated), 172mg cholesterol, 1,400mg sodium.

Pad Thai

Thai Shrimp

Ginger, lime, and cilantro lend exotic flavor to this easy weeknight entrée. Spoon over jasmine rice to serve.

PREP: 30 MINUTES   COOK: 15 MINUTES
MAKES 4 MAIN-DISH SERVINGS.

2 medium limes
3 teaspoons vegetable oil
1 small onion, finely chopped
1 small red pepper, thinly sliced
2 teaspoons grated, peeled
   fresh ginger
1/8 to 1/4 teaspoon ground red pepper
   (cayenne)
4 ounces medium mushrooms,
   trimmed and each cut into quarters

1/2 teaspoon salt
1 can (13 3/4 to 15 ounces) light
   coconut milk (not cream of
   coconut; see Tip below)
1 pound large shrimp, shelled
   and deveined
2 ounces snow peas, strings removed
   and cut into matchstick-thin strips
1/3 cups loosely packed fresh
   cilantro leaves

1. With vegetable peeler, peel six 1" by 3/4" strips of peel from limes, then squeeze 2 tablespoons juice.

2. In nonstick 12-inch skillet, heat 2 teaspoons oil over medium heat until hot. Add onion and cook until tender, about 5 minutes. Add sliced red pepper and cook 1 minute. Stir in ginger and ground red pepper; cook 1 minute. Transfer onion mixture to small bowl.

3. In same skillet, heat remaining 1 teaspoon oil over medium-high heat until hot. Add mushrooms and salt and cook until tender, and lightly browned, about 3 minutes. Add coconut milk, lime peel, lime juice, and onion mixture, and heat to boiling. Add shrimp and cook until shrimp turn opaque throughout. Stir in snow peas; heat through. Stir in cilantro.

Each serving: About 425 calories, 25g protein, 47g carbohydrate, 14g total fat (6g saturated), 142mg cholesterol, 420mg sodium.

Tip

Coconut milk is available in Asian or Hispanic grocery stores and some supermarkets.

Shrimp Étouffée

This popular Cajun dish features shrimp smothered in a thick, spicy sauce. For faster preparation, we call for a bag of frozen shrimp.

PREP: 15 MINUTES   COOK: 25 MINUTES
MAKES 4 MAIN-DISH SERVINGS.

1 cup regular long-grain white rice
1/4 cup all-purpose flour
2 tablespoons olive oil
1 small onion, cut into 1/4-inch pieces
1 stalk celery, cut into 1/4-inch pieces
1/2 small green pepper, cut into 1/4-inch pieces
1/2 teaspoon salt
1/2 teaspoon dried basil

1/4 teaspoon ground red pepper (cayenne)
1/4 teaspoon coarsely ground black pepper
1/4 teaspoon dried thyme
1 bottle (8 ounces) clam juice
3/4 cup water
1 bag (16 ounces) frozen raw, shelled, and deveined large shrimp
2 green onions, trimmed and chopped

1. Prepare rice as label directs.
2. Meanwhile, in nonstick 10-inch skillet, cook flour over medium-high heat, stirring and shaking pan frequently, until flour turns a nutty brown, 6 to 8 minutes. Transfer flour to small bowl; set aside. Wipe skillet clean.
3. In same skillet, heat oil over medium heat until hot. Add onion, celery, green pepper, salt, basil, ground red pepper, black pepper, and thyme, and cook, stirring often, until vegetables are tender, about 10 minutes.
4. Increase heat to medium-high. Sprinkle cooked flour over vegetable mixture; stir until blended. Gradually stir in clam juice and water, whisking constantly, and heat to boiling; boil 1 minute. Add shrimp and cook until shrimp turn opaque throughout, 3 to 4 minutes longer. Serve shrimp mixture over rice; garnish with green onions.

Each serving: About 395 calories, 28g protein, 48g carbohydrate, 9g total fat (1g saturated), 174mg cholesterol, 600mg sodium.

Sesame Shrimp & Asparagus Stir-Fry

If fresh asparagus is not available, this is also delicious with green beans; stir-fry beans for 5 minutes.

PREP: 5 MINUTES   COOK: 20 MINUTES
MAKES 4 MAIN-DISH SERVINGS.

1 cup regular long-grain white rice
2 tablespoons soy sauce
1 tablespoon seasoned rice vinegar
1 tablespoon grated, peeled
   fresh ginger
1 tablespoon sesame seeds

2 teaspoons vegetable oil
1 pound asparagus, trimmed and cut
   diagonally into 2-inch pieces
1 pint cherry tomatoes
1 pound cooked large shrimp, shelled
1 teaspoon Asian sesame oil

1. Prepare rice as label directs.

2. Meanwhile, in cup, with fork, stir soy sauce, rice vinegar, and ginger; set aside.

3. In nonstick 12-inch skillet, toast sesame seeds over medium-high heat until golden, about 4 minutes. Transfer to small bowl.

4. In same skillet, heat vegetable oil over medium–high heat until hot. Add asparagus and cook, stirring frequently, until tender-crisp, about 5 minutes. Add cherry tomatoes and cook, stirring frequently, 2 minutes. Stir soy-sauce mixture and shrimp into asparagus mixture; cook until heated through, about 1 minute. Remove skillet from heat; stir in sesame oil.

5. To serve, spoon rice onto 4 dinner plates; top with shrimp mixture and sprinkle with sesame seeds.

Each serving: About 370 calories, 31g protein, 45g carbohydrate, 7g total fat (1g saturated), 221mg cholesterol, 880mg sodium.

Sesame Shrimp & Asparagus Stir-Fry

Shrimp with Mint Orzo

Serve by the bowlful when you want to indulge. The no-cook sauce, laced with delicate dill and fresh mint, is perfect with shrimp and feta cheese.

PREP: 25 MINUTES   COOK: 20 MINUTES
MAKES 4 MAIN-DISH SERVINGS.

1 1/2 cups orzo (rice-shaped pasta)
1 bay leaf
2 tablespoons olive oil
1 pound medium shrimp, shelled and deveined, each cut crosswise into 3 pieces
1/2 teaspoon salt
1 ripe large tomato, chopped
1 medium red onion, finely chopped
3/4 cup crumbled feta cheese (3 ounces)

1/2 cup loosely packed fresh parsley leaves, chopped
1 tablespoon plus 2 teaspoons fresh lemon juice
2 tablespoons chopped fresh mint leaves
1 tablespoon chopped fresh dill
1/8 teaspoon ground red pepper (cayenne)

1. Prepare orzo as label directs, but add bay leaf.

2. Meanwhile, in nonstick 12-inch skillet, heat 1 tablespoon olive oil over medium-high heat until hot. Add shrimp and 1/4 teaspoon salt, and cook until shrimp turn opaque throughout, 2 to 3 minutes. Spoon shrimp into large bowl.

3. Drain orzo; discard bay leaf. Add orzo to bowl with shrimp; gently stir in tomato, onion, feta, parsley, lemon juice, mint, dill, ground red pepper, remaining 1 tablespoon oil, and remaining 1/4 teaspoon salt. Serve at room temperature.

Each serving: About 475 calories, 31g protein, 55g carbohydrate, 14g total fat (5g saturated), 161mg cholesterol, 720mg sodium.

Pesto Shrimp with Orzo & Rice

With store-bought pesto, this dish is a snap to prepare. Cook shrimp quickly over a bed of orzo pilaf, then stir in fragrant basil sauce.

PREP: 10 MINUTES   COOK: 30 MINUTES

MAKES 4 MAIN-DISH SERVINGS.

1/2 cup orzo (rice-shaped pasta)
3/4 cup regular long-grain white rice
1/2 teaspoon salt
2 1/2 cups water
1 pound shelled and deveined
   medium shrimp

1/4 cup refrigerated store-bought
   basil pesto
1/2 cup loosely packed fresh basil or
   parsley leaves, chopped
lemon wedges

1. In nonstick 12-inch skillet, toast orzo over medium-high heat, shaking skillet frequently, until orzo is golden. Add rice, salt, and water; heat to boiling. Reduce heat to low; cover and simmer 20 minutes.

2. Arrange shrimp over orzo mixture; cover and cook until shrimp turn opaque throughout, 2 to 4 minutes. Stir in pesto; sprinkle with basil or parsley. Serve with lemon wedges.

Each serving: About 405 calories, 30g protein, 46g carbohydrate, 10g total fat (2g saturated), 178mg cholesterol, 550mg sodium.

Shrimp Fra Diavolo

Shrimp is simmered in a devilishly spicy tomato sauce with garlic and onion, then tossed with spaghetti.

PREP: 5 MINUTES   COOK: 16 MINUTES
MAKES 6 MAIN-DISH SERVINGS.

1 package (16 ounces) thin
  spaghetti
1 tablespoon olive oil
1 medium onion, chopped
2 garlic cloves, crushed with
  garlic press
1/4 teaspoon crushed red pepper

1 can (28 ounces) whole tomatoes
1/2 teaspoon salt
1 pound shelled and deveined
  large shrimp
1/4 cup loosely packed fresh parsley
  leaves, chopped

1. In large covered saucepot, cook pasta as label directs.

2. Meanwhile, in nonstick 12-inch skillet, heat oil over medium heat. Add onion and cook, covered, stirring often, until tender and golden, about 5 minutes. Add garlic and crushed red pepper; cook 1 minute.

3. Add tomatoes with their juice and 1/2 teaspoon salt; heat to boiling over medium-high heat, breaking up tomatoes with side of spoon. Reduce heat to medium, and cook, covered, 5 minutes. Stir in shrimp, and cook, covered, until shrimp turn opaque throughout, about 5 minutes.

4. Drain pasta; return to saucepot. Add shrimp mixture; toss to combine. Sprinkle with parsley.

Each serving: About 415 calories, 27g protein, 65g carbohydrate, 5g total fat (1g saturated), 115mg cholesterol, 605mg sodium.

Shrimp Curry with Peas

For an extra flourish, you can serve this dish the traditional way—with small dishes of peanuts, shredded coconut, and plain yogurt to sprinkle on top.

PREP: 10 MINUTES   COOK: 20 MINUTES
MAKES 4 MAIN-DISH SERVINGS.

1 cup regular long-grain white rice
1 tablespoon olive oil
1 large sweet onion (12 ounces; such as Texas SuperSweet or Walla Walla), cut in half and thinly sliced
2 garlic cloves, crushed with garlic press
1 tablespoon grated, peeled fresh ginger
2 teaspoons ground coriander
2 teaspoons ground cumin
1/2 teaspoon salt
1/8 teaspoon ground red pepper (cayenne)
2 large tomatoes (1 pound), coarsely chopped
1 pound shelled and deveined large shrimp
1 cup frozen peas
1/2 cup coarsely chopped fresh cilantro leaves and stems
1/4 cup sweetened flaked coconut

1. Prepare rice as label directs.
2. Meanwhile, in nonstick 12-inch skillet, heat oil over medium-high heat until hot. Add onion and cook until soft, 8 to 10 minutes. Stir in garlic, ginger, coriander, cumin, salt, and ground red pepper; cook, stirring, 1 minute.
3. Add tomatoes with any juice to skillet, and cook 3 minutes. Stir in shrimp; cover and cook, stirring occasionally, just until shrimp turn opaque throughout, 3 minutes. Add peas, cilantro, and coconut; cover and cook until heated through, about 1 minute.
4. To serve, spoon rice onto 4 dinner plates; top with shrimp curry.

Each serving: About 420 calories, 30g protein, 55g carbohydrate, 8g total fat (2g saturated), 172mg cholesterol, 520mg sodium.

Coconut Shrimp Curry

This dish tastes as good as classic slow-cooking curry but is ready in a flash. Serve with crisp flat breads such as pappadams.

PREP: 10 MINUTES   COOK: 20 MINUTES
MAKES 4 MAIN-DISH SERVINGS.

1 cup regular long-grain rice
2 teaspoons olive oil
1 medium onion, chopped
1 tablespoon curry powder
1 teaspoon mustard seeds
1 pound shelled and deveined fresh or frozen (thawed) large shrimp, with tail part of shell left on if you like

1/2 cup light coconut milk (not cream of coconut) (see Tip page 134)
3/4 cup frozen peas, thawed
1 cup frozen whole baby carrots, thawed
1/2 teaspoon salt
chopped fresh cilantro leaves (optional)

1. Prepare rice as label directs but do not add butter or margarine.

2. Meanwhile, in nonstick 12-inch skillet, heat 1 teaspoon olive oil over medium-high heat until hot. Reduce heat to medium; add onion and cook until tender, about 8 minutes. Add curry powder and cook, stirring, 1 minute. Transfer onion mixture to medium bowl.

3. Increase heat to medium-high. In same skillet, heat remaining 1 teaspoon oil until hot. Add mustard seeds; cook, stirring, 30 seconds. Add shrimp and cook, stirring frequently, until opaque throughout, about 4 minutes.

4. Return onion mixture to skillet; stir in coconut milk, peas, carrots, and salt; cook until heated through. Serve over rice. Sprinkle with cilantro, if you like.

Each serving: About 390 calories, 30g protein, 49g carbohydrate, 8g total fat (2g saturated), 175mg cholesterol, 490mg sodium.

Jambalaya

A Cajun favorite, jambalaya is a rice dish with countless variations. The two constants, however, are pork and shellfish.

PREP: 10 MINUTES   COOK: 20 MINUTES
MAKES 4 MAIN-DISH SERVINGS.

1 package (3 1/2 to 4 ounces)
   sliced chorizo sausage, cut into
   1/4-inch-wide strips
2 garlic cloves, crushed with
   garlic press
2 stalks celery, thinly sliced
1 medium onion, chopped

1 can (14 1/2 ounces) diced tomatoes
1 1/2 cups instant brown rice
1/2 teaspoon salt
1 1/2 cups water
8 ounces cleaned and cooked
   large shrimp

1. In nonstick 12-inch skillet, cook chorizo, garlic, celery, and onion over medium-high heat until celery is tender, 10 to 12 minutes.
2. Stir in tomatoes with their juice, rice, salt, and water; heat to boiling over high heat. Reduce heat to medium-low; cover and simmer until rice is tender, 8 to 10 minutes. Stir in shrimp; cover and cook until heated through, about 1 minute.

Each serving: About 320 calories, 23g protein, 33g carbohydrate, 11g total fat (4g saturated), 132mg cholesterol, 1,150mg sodium.

Tip

You may want to drizzle with hot sauce, depending on how spicy the sausages are. For a more traditional jambalaya, add 4 ounces cut-up cooked chicken along with the shrimp.

Paella Pronto

Paella Pronto

This Spanish rice dish is named for the large, flat pan with low sides in which it is traditionally prepared and served. A heavy nonstick skillet also works fine.

PREP: 10 MINUTES   COOK: 25 MINUTES
MAKES 4 MAIN-DISH SERVINGS.

2 hot Italian-sausage links (about
  6 ounces), casings removed
1 cup regular long-grain rice
1/2 teaspoon salt
2 1/2 cups water

1 (14 1/2- to 16-ounce) can
  stewed tomatoes
1 pound large shrimp, shelled and
  deveined, with tail part of shell left on
1 cup frozen peas, thawed

1. Heat nonstick 10-inch skillet over medium-high heat until hot. Add sausage and cook, breaking up sausage using side of spoon, until browned. With slotted spoon, transfer sausage to bowl.

2. Reduce heat to medium. Add rice to drippings in skillet, and cook, stirring occasionally, 2 minutes. Add salt and water; heat to boiling. Reduce heat to low; cover and simmer mixture until liquid is almost absorbed, 12 to 15 minutes.

3. Add stewed tomatoes and sausage; heat to boiling over high heat. Add shrimp; heat to boiling. Reduce heat to medium; cover and cook for 4 minutes. Stir in peas; cover and cook until shrimp turn opaque throughout and peas are heated through.

Each serving: About 460 calories, 30g protein, 51g carbohydrate, 15g total fat (4g saturated), 175mg cholesterol, 1,095mg sodium.

EGGS & CHEESE

Spinach & Feta Bread Pudding
recipe on page 170

Three Omelet Suppers

For an easy lunch or supper, nothing beats a quick-cooking omelet, and here are three of our favorites. Make the filling first so it's ready to be spooned onto the omelet.

PREP: 10 MINUTES   COOK: 5 MINUTES
MAKES 4 MAIN-DISH SERVINGS.

filling of choice (below)	1/2 teaspoon salt
8 eggs	4 teaspoons butter or margarine
1/2 cup water	

1. Prepare filling (below).
2. In large bowl, beat 8 eggs with water and salt. In nonstick 8-inch skillet melt 1 teaspoon butter over medium-high heat. Pour 1/2 cup egg mixture into skillet; cook, until set around edge, about 1 minute.
3. With heat-safe spatula, gently lift edge of eggs as they set, tilting skillet to allow uncooked egg to run underneath until eggs are set but still moist on top.
4. Spoon one-fourth of filling on half of omelet. Tilt the skillet and fold unfilled half of omelet over. Slide onto warm plate. Repeat with remaining egg mixture and filling.

Creamy Mushroom

In nonstick 10-inch skillet, heat *1 tablespoon butter* over medium-high heat. Add *1 medium onion*, minced; cook 5 minutes. Stir in *8 ounces mushrooms, trimmed and thinly sliced, 1/4 teaspoon salt*, and *1/8 teaspoon black pepper*; cook until liquid has evaporated. Stir in *1/4 cup heavy cream*; boil 3 minutes. Stir in *2 tablespoons chopped parsley*.

Each serving: About 290 calories, 15g protein, 8g carbohydrate, 23g total fat (11g saturated), 463mg cholesterol, 636mg sodium.

Black Bean &
Salsa Omelet

Black Bean & Salsa

In nonstick 10-inch skillet, heat *1 cup canned black beans*, rinsed and drained, and *1 cup medium-hot salsa* over medium-high heat, stirring often, until liquid has evaporated. Divide black-bean mixture, *1 medium avocado*, peeled and diced, and *1/4 cup sour cream* among omelets.

Each serving: About 359 calories, 19g protein, 17g carbohydrate, 25g total fat (9g saturated), 442mg cholesterol, 957mg sodium.

Red Pepper & Goat Cheese

In nonstick 10-inch skillet, melt *2 teaspoons butter* over medium-high heat. Add *1 medium red pepper*, thinly sliced, and *1/4 teaspoon salt*; cook until tender and browned. Add *1 garlic clove*, minced; cook 1 minute. Divide red pepper, *2 ounces goat cheese*, and *1/2 cup packed torn arugula* among omelets.

Each serving: About 256 calories, 16g protein, 3g carbohydrate, 20g total fat (10g saturated), 451mg cholesterol, 691mg sodium.

Smoked Salmon Omelet

Perfect for a light meal, this omelet pairs prepared chive-and-onion cream cheese with slivers of rich smoked salmon.

PREP: 10 MINUTES   COOK: 5 MINUTES
MAKES 4 MAIN-DISH SERVINGS.

8 large eggs
1/2 cup water
1 tablespoon butter or margarine
4 ounces chive-and-onion
   cream cheese
4 ounces smoked salmon, cut into
   thin strips

1 medium tomato, chopped
2 tablespoons capers, drained
4 slices pumpernickel or rye bread,
   toasted

1. In large bowl, with wire whisk or fork, beat eggs with water.
2. In nonstick 12-inch skillet, melt butter over medium-high heat. Pour egg mixture into skillet; cook until set around edge, 2 to 3 minutes.
3. With heat-safe spatula, gently lift edge of eggs as they set, tilting skillet to allow uncooked eggs to run underneath until eggs are set but still moist on top.
4. Spoon cream cheese over half of omelet. Top with salmon, tomato, and capers; cook 1 minute longer. Tilt skillet and fold unfilled half of omelet over filling. Slide omelet onto warm platter. Serve with toasted bread.

Each serving: About 395 calories, 22g protein, 20g carbohydrate, 24g total fat (11g saturated), 467mg cholesterol, 846mg sodium.

Mexican Frittata

Spicy Spanish chorizo gives this delectable omelet real south-of-the-border flavor. And it takes just 5 minutes to prepare thanks to supermarket shredded hash brown potatoes.

PREP: 5 MINUTES   COOK: 15 MINUTES
MAKES 4 MAIN-DISH SERVINGS.

1 package (3 1/2 ounces) chorizo
  sausage, thinly sliced
1 small green pepper, sliced
1 medium onion, cut in half
  and sliced
1 1/2 cups refrigerated shredded hash
  brown potatoes (about half
  20-ounce bag)

6 large eggs
1/2 teaspoon salt
1/4 cup water

1. Preheat oven to 450°F. In covered nonstick 10-inch skillet with oven-safe handle (or with handle wrapped in double thickness of foil), cook chorizo, pepper, and onion over medium heat, covered, stirring occasionally, until pepper and onion are soft and lightly browned, about 10 minutes. Stir in potatoes, and cook just until heated through, about 1 minute. Spread potato mixture evenly in skillet.
2. Meanwhile, in small bowl, whisk eggs, salt, and water until blended.
3. Pour egg mixture into skillet over potato mixture; do not stir. Place skillet in oven, and bake until set, 5 to 6 minutes.
4. To serve, loosen frittata from skillet, and slide onto warm platter. Cut into wedges.

Each serving: About 300 calories, 18g protein, 19g carbohydrate, 17g total fat (6g saturated), 341mg cholesterol, 730mg sodium.

Bacon, Cheddar & Pea Frittata

Bacon, Cheddar & Pea Frittata

The kids will especially love a skillet omelet made with Cheddar and bacon filling—they'll even eat the peas!

PREP: 15 MINUTES   BAKE: 10 MINUTES
MAKES 4 MAIN-DISH SERVINGS.

FRITTATA MIXTURE
6 large eggs
1/4 cup milk
1/4 teaspoon coarsely ground black
  pepper

FILLING
4 slices bacon, cut into
  1/4-inch pieces
1 cup frozen peas, thawed
2 ounces sharp Cheddar cheese,
  shredded (1/2 cup)

1. Preheat oven to 350°F.

2. Prepare frittata mixture: In large bowl, with wire whisk or fork, beat eggs with milk and pepper until blended; set aside.

3. Prepare filling: In nonstick 10-inch skillet with oven-safe handle (or with handle wrapped in double thickness of foil), cook bacon over medium heat until browned, stirring frequently, about 5 minutes. Pour off drippings from skillet, leaving bacon. Stir in peas, and cook 1 minute.

4. Reduce heat to medium-low. Pour egg mixture over filling in skillet; sprinkle top evenly with cheese. Cook, without stirring, until egg mixture begins to set around edge, about 3 minutes. Place skillet in oven, and bake until set, 10 to 12 minutes.

5. To serve, loosen frittata from skillet and slide onto warm platter. Cut into wedges.

Each serving: About 305 calories, 22g protein, 8g carbohydrate, 21g total fat (10g saturated), 357mg cholesterol, 415mg sodium.

Frittata Lorraine

The classic ingredients of a quiche Lorraine—bacon and Gruyère cheese—without the crust make this dish a favorite weeknight meal.

PREP: 30 MINUTES   BAKE: 10 MINUTES
MAKES 4 MAIN-DISH SERVINGS.

3 slices bacon
2 medium all-purpose potatoes
  (about 12 ounces), peeled and
  coarsely shredded
1 medium onion, chopped
1/2 teaspoon salt
4 large eggs

4 large egg whites
2 ounces Gruyère cheese, shredded
  (1/2 cup)
1/4 teaspoon coarsely ground
  black pepper
1/3 cup water

1. In nonstick 10-inch skillet with oven-safe handle (or with handle wrapped in double thickness of foil), cook bacon over medium heat until browned. Transfer bacon to paper towels to drain; crumble bacon. Discard all but 1 tablespoon bacon drippings.

2. To skillet with drippings, add shredded potatoes, onion, and 1/4 teaspoon salt, and cook, stirring occasionally, until vegetables are tender and golden, about 15 minutes.

3. Meanwhile, preheat oven to 400°F. In medium bowl, with wire whisk or fork, beat eggs and egg whites with bacon, cheese, pepper, remaining 1/4 teaspoon salt, and water. Stir egg mixture into potato mixture in skillet and cook over medium heat, covered, until egg mixture begins to set around edge, about 5 minutes. Remove cover and place skillet in oven; bake until set, about 10 minutes.

4. To serve, loosen frittata from skillet, and slide onto warm platter. Cut into wedges.

Each serving: About 275 calories, 17g protein, 17g carbohydrate, 15g total fat (6g saturated), 235mg cholesterol, 535mg sodium.

Chive & Goat Cheese Frittata

With dollops of melted cheese on top, this frittata is sure to please. Fontina can be substituted for the goat cheese, if you prefer.

PREP: 10 MINUTES   BAKE: 10 MINUTES
MAKES 4 MAIN-DISH SERVINGS.

8 large eggs
1/2 cup milk
1/2 teaspoon salt
1/8 teaspoon coarsely ground
  black pepper
1 medium tomato, finely chopped

2 tablespoons chopped fresh chives
2 teaspoons butter or margarine
1/2 (5 1/4-ounce) package goat
  cheese or 3 ounces shredded
  Fontina cheese

1. Preheat oven to 375°F. In medium bowl, with wire whisk or fork, mix eggs, milk, salt, and pepper. Stir in tomato and chives.

2. In nonstick 10-inch skillet with oven-safe handle (or with handle wrapped in double thickness of foil), melt butter over medium heat. Pour in egg mixture; drop spoonfuls of goat cheese on top of eggs. Cook until frittata begins to set around edge, 3 to 4 minutes.

3. Place skillet in oven; bake until set and knife inserted in center comes out clean, 9 to 10 minutes.

4. To serve, loosen frittata from skillet, and slide onto warm platter. Cut into wedges.

Each serving: About 240 calories, 17g protein, 4g carbohydrate, 17g total fat (7g saturated), 443mg cholesterol, 502mg sodium.

Asparagus & Green-Onion Frittata

Everyone loves a skillet omelet, especially when it's filled with bits of cream cheese and sautéed vegetables.

PREP: 25 MINUTES   BAKE: 10 MINUTES
MAKES 4 MAIN-DISH SERVINGS.

8 large eggs
1/2 cup whole milk
1/8 teaspoon ground black pepper
3/4 teaspoon salt
12 ounces asparagus, trimmed

1 tablespoon butter or margarine
1 bunch green onions, trimmed
  and chopped
2 ounces light cream cheese
  (Neufchâtel)

1. Preheat oven to 375°F. In medium bowl, with wire whisk or fork, mix eggs, milk, pepper, and 1/2 teaspoon salt until blended; set aside. If using thin asparagus, cut each stalk crosswise in half; if using medium asparagus, cut stalks into 1-inch pieces.

2. In nonstick 10-inch skillet with oven-safe handle (or with handle wrapped in double thickness of foil), melt butter over medium heat. Add asparagus and remaining 1/4 teaspoon salt, and cook, stirring often, 4 minutes for thin stalks or 6 minutes for medium-size stalks. Stir in green onions, and cook, stirring occasionally, until the vegetables are tender, 2 to 3 minutes longer.

3. Reduce heat to medium-low. Pour egg mixture over vegetables in skillet; drop scant teaspoonfuls of cream cheese on top of egg mixture. Cook, without stirring, until egg mixture begins to set around edge, 3 to 4 minutes. Place skillet in oven, and bake until set and knife inserted in center comes out clean, 10 to 12 minutes.

4. To serve, loosen frittata from skillet, and slide onto warm platter. Cut into wedges.

Each serving: About 250 calories, 17g protein, 6g carbohydrate, 18g total fat (7g saturated), 448mg cholesterol, 671mg sodium.

Asparagus & Green-Onion Frittata

Eggs Florentine

This slimmed-down recipe is every bit as satisfying as the calorie-laden classic. And with precooked polenta, it's easier to make, too.

PREP: 25 MINUTES   BAKE: 20 MINUTES
MAKES 6 MAIN-DISH SERVINGS.

1 log (16 ounces) precooked polenta
6 slices Canadian-style bacon (about 4 ounces)
1 1/2 cups low-fat (1%) milk
1 tablespoon cornstarch
1/2 teaspoon salt
pinch ground red pepper (cayenne)

1/2 cup water
1 package (10 ounces) frozen chopped spinach, thawed and squeezed dry
1/4 cup grated Parmesan cheese
6 large eggs

1. Preheat oven to 400°F. Grease shallow 2 1/2-quart casserole. Cut polenta log crosswise in half, then cut each half lengthwise into 3 slices. Place polenta slices in single layer in casserole; bake until heated through, about 15 minutes. Top each polenta slice with 1 slice bacon; return to oven, and bake 5 minutes longer. Keep warm.

2. Meanwhile, in 2-quart saucepan, with wire whisk, mix milk, cornstarch, salt, ground red pepper, and water until well blended. Cook over medium-high heat until mixture thickens and boils; boil, stirring, 1 minute. Stir in spinach and Parmesan; cook until heated through.

3. Poach eggs: In 12-inch skillet, heat *1 1/2 inches water* to boiling over medium-high heat. Reduce heat to medium-low. Break cold eggs, one at a time, into small cup; holding cup close to surface of water, slip each egg into simmering water. Cook eggs, until whites have set and yolks begin to thicken, 3 to 5 minutes. With slotted spoon, carefully remove eggs, one at a time, from water, and very briefly drain (still held in slotted spoon) on paper towels.

Eggs Florentine

4. To serve, place 1 bacon-topped polenta slice on each of 6 plates. Spoon spinach mixture over bacon and polenta; top each with a poached egg. Serve immediately.

Each serving: About 215 calories, 16g protein, 18g carbohydrate, 8g total fat (3g saturated), 226mg cholesterol, 995mg sodium.

Egg & Black-Bean Burritos

Scrambled eggs with a sprinkling of Monterey Jack are wrapped in flour tortillas with black beans and salsa—like the popular takeout, only better—and it's on the table in just 15 minutes!

PREP: 10 MINUTES   COOK: 5 MINUTES
MAKES 4 MAIN-DISH SERVINGS.

1 can (15 to 19 ounces) black beans, rinsed and drained
1 jar (11 ounces) medium-hot salsa (about 1 1/4 cups)
6 large eggs
1/4 teaspoon salt

1/8 teaspoon coarsely ground black pepper
4 ounces shredded Monterey Jack cheese (1 cup)
4 (10-inch) flour tortillas

1. In small microwave-safe bowl, mix black beans with salsa; set aside. In medium bowl, with wire whisk or fork, beat the eggs, salt, and pepper until blended.

2. Heat nonstick 10-inch skillet over medium-high heat until hot. Pour egg mixture into skillet. As egg mixture begins to set, with heat-safe rubber spatula or wooden spoon, stir egg mixture lightly to allow uncooked egg mixture to flow toward side of pan. Cook until edges are set to desired doness, 4 to 6 minutes longer. Remove skillet from heat; sprinkle cheese evenly over eggs.

3. Meanwhile, in microwave oven, heat black-bean mixture on High, stirring once, until heated through, 1 to 2 minutes. Cover and keep warm.

4. Stack tortillas and place between 2 damp microwave-safe paper towels. In microwave oven, heat tortillas on High until warm, about 1 minute.

5. For each burrito, spoon one-fourth of scrambled eggs down center of tortilla; top with about one-fourth of black-bean mixture. Fold two opposite sides of tortilla over filling, then fold over remaining two sides to form a package.

Each serving: About 575 calories, 28g protein, 71g carbohydrate, 21g total fat (9g saturated), 344mg cholesterol, 1,550mg sodium.

Greens & Ricotta Pie

It's like a quiche without the crust! Swiss chard and green onions make up this savory dish—an easy entrée for supper or brunch.

PREP: 30 MINUTES   BAKE: 40 MINUTES
MAKES 6 MAIN-DISH SERVINGS.

1 large head Swiss chard (about
  1 3/4 pounds)
1 tablespoon olive oil
1 bunch green onions, trimmed and
  cut into 1/4-inch-thick slices
1/2 teaspoon salt
1/4 teaspoon coarsely ground
  black pepper

4 large eggs
1 container (15 ounces) part-skim
  ricotta cheese
3/4 cup low-fat (1%) milk
1/2 cup grated Parmesan cheese
2 tablespoons cornstarch

1. Preheat oven to 350°F. Grease 9 1/2-inch deep-dish glass pie plate.

2. Trim 2 inches from Swiss-chard stems; discard ends. Separate stems from leaves; thinly slice stems, and coarsely chop leaves.

3. In nonstick 12-inch skillet, heat oil over medium-high heat until hot. Add sliced stems and cook, stirring frequently, until tender and lightly browned, about 4 minutes. Add green onions, salt, and pepper, and cook 1 minute. Gradually add chopped chard leaves, and cook, stirring, until wilted and excess moisture has evaporated, about 5 minutes.

4. In large bowl, with wire whisk or fork, mix eggs, ricotta, milk, Parmesan, and cornstarch. Stir in Swiss-chard mixture. Transfer mixture to prepared pie plate. Bake pie until knife inserted 2 inches from center comes out clean, about 40 minutes.

Each serving: About 255 calories, 19g protein, 14g carbohydrate, 14g total fat (7g saturated), 172mg cholesterol, 680mg sodium.

Egg Foo Yong Oven Pancake

Egg Foo Yong Oven Pancake

Our take on the classic Chinese restaurant item calls for ramen noodles, mushrooms, eggs, and flavorful seasonings.

PREP: 30 MINUTES   BAKE: 10 MINUTES
MAKES 4 MAIN-DISH SERVINGS.

2 packages (3 ounces each) ramen
  noodle soup mix (any flavor)
6 large eggs
2 teaspoons Asian sesame oil
1 teaspoon sugar
3/4 teaspoon salt
1 tablespoon vegetable oil
1 medium stalk celery, trimmed, cut
  lengthwise in half, and then thinly
  sliced crosswise

3 green onions, trimmed and
  thinly sliced
1 package (8 ounces) sliced
  mushrooms
2 tablespoons grated, peeled
  fresh ginger
soy sauce (optional)

1. Preheat oven to 350°F. In nonstick 12-inch skillet with oven-safe handle (or with handle wrapped in double thickness of foil), heat *4 cups water* to boiling over medium-high heat. Break up noodles into large pieces (discard seasoning packets or save for another use); add to skillet and cook, stirring occasionally, 3 minutes. Drain noodles. Wipe skillet dry.

2. In large bowl, with fork or wire whisk, beat eggs, sesame oil, sugar, and salt until blended. Stir in cooked noodles; set aside.

3. In same skillet, heat vegetable oil over medium-high heat until hot. Add celery and cook, stirring occasionally, 2 minutes. Reserve 2 tablespoons green onions for garnish. Add mushrooms, ginger, and remaining green onions, and cook until mushroom are lightly browned, about 8 minutes. Stir mushrooms mixture into noodle mixture in bowl.

4. Reduce heat to medium. Add the noodle mixture to skillet, and spread into an even layer; cook 2 minutes. Place skillet in oven; bake until pancake is set, 8 to 10 minutes.

5. To serve, invert skillet onto cutting board. Remove skillet and cut pancake into wedges. Sprinkle with reserved green onions. Serve with soy sauce, if you like.

Each serving: About 370 calories, 15g protein, 34g carbohydrate, 20g total fat (3g saturated), 320mg cholesterol, 550mg sodium.

Three-Cheese Polenta Pizza

Slice a log of store-bought polenta, sauté in olive oil, then top with cheeses and a mixture of diced tomatoes and fresh basil. Look for polenta near the cheese aisle in the supermarket.

Prep: 15 minutes Cook: 20 minutes
Makes 6 main-dish servings.

2 teaspoons olive oil
1 package (24 ounces) precooked polenta, cut crosswise into 12 slices
1 cup part-skim ricotta cheese
1/2 cup shredded part-skim mozzarella cheese (2 ounces)
1/4 cup grated Parmesan cheese

1/2 teaspoon salt
1/4 teaspoon coarsely ground black pepper
1/2 cup loosely packed fresh basil leaves, sliced
8 medium plum tomatoes (about 1 1/2 pounds), cut into 1/4-inch pieces

1. In nonstick 12-inch skillet, heat oil over medium-high heat until hot. Arrange polenta rounds in even layer in skillet, and cook until lightly browned on both sides, about 15 minutes.

2. Meanwhile, in medium bowl, mix ricotta, mozzarella, Parmesan, 1/4 teaspoon salt, and pepper until blended. Reserve 1 tablespoon sliced basil for garnish. In another medium bowl, toss tomatoes with remaining basil and remaining 1/4 teaspoon salt.

3. Reduce heat to medium; spoon ricotta mixture over polenta slices in skillet and top with tomato mixture. Cover skillet and cook until hot and cheese has melted, about 5 minutes. Sprinkle with reserved basil.

Each serving: About 220 calories, 12g protein, 25g carbohydrate, 8g total fat (4g saturated), 23mg cholesterol, 745mg sodium.

Three-Cheese Polenta Pizza

Poblano Rigatoni

Poblano Rigatoni

Forget the grill. You'll get the same char-roasted flavor by searing the poblanos in a hot skillet (and you won't have to peel the chiles either!).

PREP: 15 MINUTES   COOK: 15 MINUTES
MAKES 4 MAIN-DISH SERVINGS.

1 package (16 ounces) rigatoni pasta
1 tablespoon olive oil
3 poblano chiles (8 ounces) or
  2 large green peppers, cut into
  1/2-inch-wide strips
1 small onion, cut into 1/2-inch-thick
  slices
2 small zucchini (about 6 ounces
  each), cut into 1/2-inch-thick slices

2 garlic cloves, crushed with garlic
  press
1 teaspoon salt
1/2 teaspoon dried oregano, crushed
1 pint grape or cherry tomatoes
4 ounces Monterey Jack cheese, cut
  into 1/2-inch cubes

1. In large saucepot, cook pasta as label directs.

2. Meanwhile, in nonstick 12-inch skillet, heat oil over medium-high heat. Add chiles and onion; cook until lightly charred and tender-crisp, about 7 minutes. Add zucchini; cover and cook 3 minutes. Add garlic, salt, and oregano; cook 30 seconds. Stir in tomatoes; cover and cook until slightly softened.

3. Drain pasta. In serving bowl, toss pasta with vegetables and cheese.

Each serving: About 635 calories, 25g protein, 100g carbohydrate, 15g total fat (7g saturated), 30mg cholesterol, 925mg sodium.

Eggs in Spicy Tomato Sauce

This classic Italian dish pairs an easy homemade tomato sauce with eggs poached right in the sauce—a delicious one-skillet dish to add to your quick-cook repertoire.

PREP: 15 MINUTES   COOK: 30 MINUTES
MAKES 4 MAIN-DISH SERVINGS.

1 loaf (8 ounces) Italian bread
1 tablespoon olive oil
1 jumbo onion (1 pound), cut into
  1/4-inch pieces
2 medium carrots, peeled and cut
  into 1/4-inch pieces
1 stalk celery, cut into
  1/4-inch pieces
2 garlic cloves, crushed with garlic
  press

1 can (28 ounces) whole tomatoes
  in juice
1/2 teaspoon salt
1/4 teaspoon crushed red pepper
1 tablespoon butter or margarine
8 large eggs
1/4 cup loosely packed fresh basil
  leaves, chopped

1. Cut bread diagonally into 1-inch-thick slices. Toast bread slices; set them aside.

2. In nonstick 12-inch skillet, heat oil over medium-high heat until hot. Add onion, carrots, celery, and garlic; cook, stirring occasionally, until vegetables are lightly browned, 12 to 15 minutes.

3. Stir in tomatoes with their juice, salt, and crushed red pepper, breaking up tomatoes with side of spoon; heat to boiling over medium-high heat. Reduce the heat to low; simmer, stirring occasionally, 5 minutes. Stir in the butter.

4. Break 1 egg into small cup. With back of spoon, make small well in sauce, and, holding cup close to surface of sauce, slip egg into well. Repeat with remaining eggs. Heat sauce to boiling over medium-high heat. Reduce heat to medium-low; cover skillet and simmer until whites have set and yolks begin to thicken, 7 to 10 minutes.

5. To serve, place 1 bread slice in each of 4 large soup bowls. Spoon 2 eggs and some tomato mixture over each slice; sprinkle with basil. Serve with remaining bread.

Each serving: About 455 calories, 21g protein, 52g carbohydrate, 19g total fat (6g saturated), 433mg cholesterol, 1,091mg sodium.

Potato Pancake with Broccoli & Cheddar

We added broccoli and Cheddar cheese to classic potato pancake to make a complete meal in a skillet.

PREP: 5 MINUTES   COOK: 20 MINUTES
MAKES 4 MAIN-DISH SERVINGS.

1 tablespoon butter or margarine
1 medium onion, chopped
1 bag (12 ounces) broccoli flowerets, each cut in half if large
1 teaspoon salt
2 tablespoons water
1 bag (20 ounces) refrigerated shredded hash brown potatoes (4 cups)

$1/8$ teaspoon ground black pepper
1 tablespoon vegetable oil
1 package (4 ounces) shredded sharp Cheddar cheese

1. In nonstick 12-inch skillet, melt butter over medium heat. Add onion and cook, stirring frequently, until browned and tender, about 5 minutes. Stir in broccoli, $1/4$ teaspoon salt, and water; cover and cook, stirring once, until broccoli is tender, about 3 minutes. Transfer broccoli mixture to medium bowl.

2. In large bowl, combine potatoes, pepper, and remaining $3/4$ teaspoon salt. In same skillet, heat oil over medium-high heat until hot. Add half the potato mixture; pat gently with rubber spatula to cover bottom of skillet. Leaving 1-inch border, top potatoes with broccoli mixture. Sprinkle Cheddar over broccoli. Cover cheese with remaining potatoes, patting to edge of skillet. Cook until browned, about 5 minutes.

3. Place large round platter or cookie sheet upside down over skillet. Grasping platter and skillet firmly together, very carefully and quickly flip skillet over to invert pancake onto platter. Slide pancake back into skillet. Cook until browned, about 5 minutes longer.

4. To serve, invert pancake onto platter and cut into wedges.

Each serving: About 350 calories, 14g protein, 40g carbohydrate, 16g total fat (8g saturated), 38mg cholesterol, 911mg sodium.

Spinach & Feta Bread Pudding

If you love the comfort of warm, sweet bread pudding for dessert, treat yourself to this savory version for brunch or supper.

PREP: 15 MINUTES PLUS STANDING   BAKE: 25 MINUTES
MAKES 6 MAIN-DISH SERVINGS.

2 tablespoons butter or margarine
1 medium onion, chopped
6 large eggs
2 cups low-fat (1%) milk
3 tablespoons chopped fresh dill
$1/2$ teaspoon freshly grated lemon peel
$1/4$ teaspoon salt
$1/4$ teaspoon coarsely ground black pepper

1 package (10 ounces) frozen chopped spinach, thawed and squeezed dry
4 ounces feta cheese, cut into $1/2$-inch cubes
8 slices firm white bread, cut into $3/4$-inch pieces

1. Preheat oven to 350°F. In nonstick 12-inch skillet with oven-safe handle (or with handle wrapped in double thickness of foil), melt butter over medium heat. Add onion and cook until tender, about 10 minutes.

2. In medium bowl, with wire whisk or fork, beat eggs, milk, dill, lemon peel, salt, and pepper until blended. With rubber spatula, stir in onion, spinach, and cheese. Gently stir in bread pieces. Pour mixture into skillet; let stand 15 minutes to allow bread to absorb liquid.

3. Cook mixture over medium-high heat, without stirring, until mixture begins to set around edge, about 3 minutes. Place skillet in oven; bake until knife inserted in center comes out clean, 20 to 25 minutes.

4. Remove pudding from oven; let stand 5 minutes before serving. To serve, cut into wedges.

Each serving: About 295 calories, 16g protein, 25g carbohydrate, 15g total fat (8g saturated), 243mg cholesterol, 643mg sodium.

Spinach & Feta Bread Pudding

Mushroom & Gruyère Rösti

This Swiss favorite is typically made with shredded potatoes that are formed into a pancake and cooked until golden and crisp on both sides. We used two layers of white rice (short grain is best because it holds together so well), with a layer of melted Gruyère cheese and sautéed mushrooms in between.

PREP: 15 MINUTES   COOK: 40 MINUTES
MAKES 6 MAIN-DISH SERVINGS.

1 1/3 cups short-grain white rice
2 2/3 cups water
1 teaspoon salt
4 teaspoons butter or margarine
1 large onion (12 ounces), finely chopped
2 ounces Gruyère cheese, shredded (1/2 cup)
8 ounces cremini and/or oyster mushrooms, trimmed and thinly sliced
8 ounces shiitake mushrooms, stems removed and caps thinly sliced
1 garlic clove, minced
1/4 teaspoon dried thyme
1/4 teaspoon coarsely ground black pepper
1/2 cup loosely packed fresh parsley leaves, chopped
1 tablespoon vegetable oil

1. In 2-quart saucepan, heat rice, water, and 3/4 teaspoon salt to boiling over high heat. Reduce heat to low; cover and simmer until rice is just tender and liquid has been absorbed, about 15 minutes.

2. Meanwhile, in nonstick 10-inch skillet, melt 2 teaspoons butter over medium heat. Add onion and cook, stirring occasionally, until tender, about 15 minutes. Stir half of cooked onion and 1/4 cup cheese into cooked rice; set aside.

3. In same skillet, melt remaining 2 teaspoons butter over medium-high heat. Add mushrooms and cook, stirring occasionally, until tender and golden, 6 to 8 minutes. Add garlic, thyme, pepper, remaining 1/4 teaspoon salt, and remaining cooked onion, and cook, stirring, 1 minute. Transfer mushroom mixture to medium bowl; stir in parsley. Reserve 1/4 cup mushroom mixture for garnish. Stir remaining 1/4 cup cheese into mushrooms in bowl.

4. In same skillet, heat 1 1/2 teaspoons oil over medium-high heat until hot; remove skillet from heat. Add half of rice mixture to skillet, and, with wide metal spatula, spread and press to form an even layer covering

Mushroom & Gruyère Rösti

bottom of skillet (rice may be sticky). Top with mushroom mixture from bowl, leaving ½-inch border of rice. Spoon remaining rice mixture over mushroom layer; press to seal rice edges together.

5. Cook rösti over medium–high heat 5 minutes; invert onto large plate (if rösti cracks or sticks to pan, press pieces back together). Add remaining 1½ teaspoons oil to skillet; slide rösti back into skillet, and cook until golden and hot, about 5 minutes longer.

6. To serve, slide rösti onto platter; top with reserved mushroom mixture. Cut into wedges.

Each serving: About 270 calories, 7g protein, 42g carbohydrate, 8g total fat (3g saturated), 13mg cholesterol, 427mg sodium.

VEGETABLES

Middle Eastern Garbanzo Beans & Macaroni
recipe on page 183

Lasagna Toss with Spinach & Ricotta

This recipe has all the flavor of a layered and baked lasagna but without the wait! Lasagna noodles are tossed with a speedy tomato-spinach skillet sauce, then dolloped with ricotta cheese to serve.

PREP: 20 MINUTES   COOK: 35 MINUTES
MAKES 4 MAIN-DISH SERVINGS.

1 package (16 ounces) lasagna noodles
1 tablespoon olive oil
1 medium onion, finely chopped
2 garlic cloves, crushed with garlic press
1 can (28 ounces) plum tomatoes in juice
3/4 teaspoon salt
1/4 teaspoon coarsely ground black pepper

1 package (10 ounces) frozen chopped spinach
1/2 cup loosely packed fresh basil leaves, chopped
1/4 cup grated Parmesan cheese plus additional for serving (optional)
1 cup part-skim ricotta cheese

1. In large saucepot, cook lasagna noodles as label directs, but increase cooking time to 12 to 14 minutes.

2. Meanwhile, in nonstick 12-inch skillet, heat oil over medium heat until hot. Add onion and cook, stirring occasionally, until tender, 10 minutes. Add garlic and cook, stirring, 30 seconds.

3. Stir in tomatoes with their juice, salt, and pepper, breaking up tomatoes with side of spoon; heat to boiling over high heat. Reduce heat to medium; cook, uncovered, 8 minutes. Add frozen spinach; cook, covered, stirring occasionally, until spinach is tender, 10 minutes. Stir in basil.

4. Drain noodles; return to saucepot. Add tomato mixture and Parmesan; toss well. Spoon into 4 pasta bowls; top with dollops of ricotta cheese. Serve with additional Parmesan, if you like.

Each serving: About 620 calories, 28g protein, 100g carbohydrate, 12g total fat (5g saturated), 23mg cholesterol, 1,640mg sodium.

Lasagna Toss with Spinach & Ricotta

Quick-Comfort Egg Noodles & Cabbage

Quick-Comfort Egg Noodles & Cabbage

Old-fashioned curly egg noodles are combined with caramelized onion, cabbage, and peas for a cozy family dinner.

PREP: 15 MINUTES   COOK: 30 MINUTES
MAKES 4 MAIN-DISH SERVINGS.

1 package (12 ounces) curly wide
  egg noodles
1 tablespoon butter or margarine
1 tablespoon olive oil
1 jumbo onion (1 pound), thinly sliced
1 small head savoy cabbage (about
  1 1/4 pounds; tough outer leaves
  discarded), trimmed, cored, and
  thinly sliced

1/4 teaspoon coarsely ground
  black pepper
1 teaspoon fresh thyme leaves or
  1/4 teaspoon dried thyme
3/4 teaspoon salt
1 package (10 ounces) frozen peas
1 cup vegetable broth
1/4 cup grated Parmesan cheese

1. In large saucepot, cook noodles as label directs.
2. Meanwhile, in nonstick 12-inch skillet, heat the butter and oil over medium heat until butter has melted. Add the onion and cook, stirring occasionally, until onion is tender and golden, 20 minutes. Increase heat to medium-high; add cabbage, pepper, thyme, and salt, and cook, stirring occasionally, until cabbage is tender-crisp and golden, about 5 minutes. Stir in frozen peas and broth; cook, stirring, 2 minutes.
3. Drain noodles; return to saucepot. Add cabbage mixture and Parmesan; toss well.

Each serving: About 540 calories, 22g protein, 88g carbohydrate, 12g total fat (4g saturated), 93mg cholesterol, 1,041mg sodium.

Polenta with Garlicky Greens

A nutritious vegetarian meal. We reduced the total prep time by microwaving the polenta. (Stir just once instead of constantly.)

PREP: 30 MINUTES   COOK: 20 MINUTES
MAKES 4 MAIN-DISH SERVINGS.

2 bunches Swiss chard (about
   3¹/₂ pounds)
1 tablespoon olive oil
3 garlic cloves, thinly sliced
¹/₄ teaspoon crushed red pepper
1¹/₄ teaspoons salt, divided
¹/₄ cup golden raisins
1¹/₂ cups yellow cornmeal

2 cups nonfat (skim) milk
¹/₃ cup plus 4 ¹/₂ cups water
2 tablespoons grated Parmesan or
   Romano cheese plus additional for
   serving (optional)
1 tablespoon pine nuts (pignoli),
   toasted and chopped

1. Trim and discard bottom 3 inches of Swiss-chard stems. Cut remaining stems into ¹/₂-inch-thick pieces; coarsely chop leaves. Rinse and dry stems and leaves separately; place in separate bowls.

2. In nonstick 12-inch skillet, heat oil, garlic, and crushed red pepper over medium heat, stirring occasionally, until garlic is lightly golden, about 2 minutes.

3. Increase heat to medium-high; add sliced chard stems to skillet, and cook, stirring occasionally, 8 minutes. Gradually add the chard leaves and ¹/₂ teaspoon salt, stirring until leaves wilt; stir in ¹/₃ cup water. Cover skillet and simmer until stems and leaves are tender, about 5 minutes. Stir in raisins; set aside.

4. Meanwhile, prepare polenta in microwave oven: In 4-quart microwave-safe bowl or casserole, combine cornmeal, remaining ³/₄ teaspoon salt, milk, and remaining 4 ¹/₂ cups water. Cover and cook on High, stirring once, until thickened, 12 to 15 minutes.

5. To serve, stir Parmesan into polenta. Spoon polenta onto platter; top with Swiss-chard mixture and sprinkle with pine nuts. Serve with additional Parmesan to sprinkle over each serving, if you like.

Each serving: About 375 calories, 16g protein, 66g carbohydrate, 6g total fat (1g saturated), 5mg cholesterol, 1,265mg sodium.

Polenta with Garlicky Greens

Tip

If you like, polenta can be prepared on stovetop: In 4-quart saucepan, stir **1 teaspoon salt** with **2 cups cold milk**. Gradually whisk in **1½ cups cornmeal** until blended, then whisk in **4½ cups boiling water**. Heat to boiling over high heat, stirring occasionally. Reduce heat to medium-low and cook, stirring frequently, partially covered, 20 minutes.

Middle Eastern Garbanzo Beans & Macaroni

Middle Eastern Garbanzo Beans & Macaroni

A flavorful stew of canned beans, crushed tomatoes, and dried spices tossed with pasta makes a satisfying vegetarian entrée.

PREP: 10 MINUTES   COOK: 35 MINUTES

MAKES 6 MAIN-DISH SERVINGS.

12 ounces macaroni twists or
  elbow macaroni
1 tablespoon olive oil
1 tablespoon butter or margarine
1 large onion, cut into 1/4-inch pieces
2 garlic cloves, crushed with
  garlic press
1 teaspoon salt
1 teaspoon ground cumin

3/4 teaspoon ground coriander
1/4 teaspoon ground allspice
1/4 teaspoon coarsely ground
  black pepper
1 can (28 ounces) crushed tomatoes
1 can (15 to 19 ounces) garbanzo
  beans, rinsed and drained
1/4 cup loosely packed fresh parsley
  leaves, chopped

1. In large saucepot, cook pasta as label directs.

2. Meanwhile, in nonstick 12-inch skillet, heat olive oil and butter over medium heat until butter has melted. Add onion and cook, stirring occasionally, until tender and golden, about 20 minutes. Stir in garlic, salt, cumin, coriander, allspice, and pepper; cook 1 minute.

3. Add tomatoes and garbanzo beans to skillet, and heat to boiling over medium-high heat. Reduce heat to medium-low; simmer, stirring occasionally, 5 minutes.

4. Drain pasta; return to saucepot. Toss garbanzo-bean mixture with pasta; heat through. Toss with chopped parsley just before serving.

Each serving: About 400 calories, 14g protein, 73g carbohydrate, 6g total fat (2g saturated), 5mg cholesterol, 1,039mg salt.

Curried Sweet Potatoes & Lentils

This hearty main dish tastes even better with a scoop of plain yogurt and a squeeze of fresh lime juice.

PREP: 15 MINUTES   COOK: 30 MINUTES
MAKES 4 MAIN-DISH SERVINGS.

1 tablespoon olive oil
1 medium onion, chopped
2 garlic cloves, minced
1 tablespoon curry powder
3 medium sweet potatoes
  (1 1/2 pounds), peeled and cut
  into 1-inch pieces

1 cup lentils, rinsed and picked over
1/2 cup regular long-grain white rice
1/2 teaspoon salt
1 can (14 1/2 ounces) vegetable broth
2 1/4 cups water
1/4 cup loosely packed fresh
  cilantro leaves

1. In nonstick 12-inch skillet, heat oil over medium heat until hot. Add onion and cook, stirring often, 5 minutes. Add garlic and curry powder, and cook, stirring constantly, 1 minute longer.

2. Stir in sweet potatoes, lentils, rice, salt, broth, and water; heat to boiling over medium heat. Reduce heat to low; cover and simmer until lentils and rice are tender and almost all liquid has been absorbed, about 30 minutes. Let stand 5 minutes. Sprinkle with cilantro to serve.

Each serving: About 460 calories, 87g carbohydrate, 5g total fat (1g saturated), 0mg cholesterol, 630mg sodium.

Curried Sweet Potatoes & Lentils

Vegetarian Chili Casserole with Corn Bread Topping

A little box of corn bread mix turns black-and-pink-bean chili into something special.

PREP: 40 MINUTES   BAKE: 20 MINUTES
MAKES 6 MAIN-DISH SERVINGS.

1 tablespoon olive oil
6 medium carrots, peeled and cut into 1/4-inch pieces
2 medium stalks celery, cut into 1/4-inch pieces
1 large onion, cut into 1/4-inch pieces
2 garlic cloves, minced
3 tablespoons chili powder
1 teaspoon ground cumin
1 can (15 ounces) crushed tomatoes in puree
1 can (15 to 19 ounces) black beans, rinsed and drained
1 can (15 1/2 to 16 ounces) pink beans, rinsed and drained
1 package (10 ounces) frozen whole-kernel corn
1 cup reduced-sodium vegetable broth
1 package (8 1/2 ounces) corn-muffin mix
1/2 cup loosely packed fresh cilantro leaves

1. Preheat oven to 400°F. In nonstick 12-inch skillet with oven-safe handle (or with handle wrapped in double thickness of foil), heat oil over medium heat until hot. Add carrots, celery, and onion; cover and cook, stirring occasionally, until vegetables are tender, about 15 minutes. Stir in garlic, chili powder, and cumin; cook, stirring, 2 minutes. Stir in tomatoes with their puree, black beans, pink beans, frozen corn, and broth; heat to boiling over high heat. Reduce heat to low; cover and simmer 5 minutes.
2. Meanwhile, prepare corn-muffin batter as label directs.
3. Top hot chili mixture in skillet with corn-muffin batter, leaving 2-inch border. Bake, uncovered, until cornbread is golden and toothpick inserted in center of topping comes out clean, 15 to 20 minutes. Sprinkle with cilantro to serve.

Each serving: About 500 calories, 20g protein, 85g carbohydrate, 11g total fat (3g saturated), 42mg cholesterol, 1,160mg sodium.

Quick Cincinnati Chili

You can put our meatless version of this Midwestern favorite together in just minutes. Then spoon it over the spaghetti straight from the skillet.

Prep: 15 minutes   Cook: 15 minutes
Makes 4 main-dish servings.

12 ounces spaghetti
2 1/4 teaspoons salt
2 teaspoons olive or vegetable oil
1 medium onion, chopped
3 tablespoons water
1 tablespoon chili powder
1/4 teaspoon ground cinnamon
1 can (15 1/2 to 16 ounces) pink
   beans, rinsed and drained

1 can (14 1/2 ounces) diced tomatoes
1/2 cup vegetable broth
1 tablespoon tomato paste
1/2 teaspoon sugar
toppings: 1/4 cup shredded reduced-
   fat Cheddar cheese, 2 tablespoons
   nonfat sour cream, 3 green onions,
   chopped

1. In large saucepan, cook spaghetti as label directs, but using 2 teaspoons salt in water. Drain and keep warm.
2. Meanwhile, in nonstick 10-inch skillet, heat oil over medium heat until hot. Add onion and water; cook until onion is tender and golden, about 10 minutes. Add chili powder and cinnamon; cook, stirring, 1 minute.
3. Stir in pink beans, tomatoes with their juice, broth, tomato paste, sugar, and remaining 1/4 teaspoon salt; heat to boiling over high heat. Reduce heat to low; simmer, uncovered, 5 minutes.
4. To serve, divide spaghetti evenly among 4 warm dinner plates. Spoon chili over spaghetti; serve with toppings.

Each serving with toppings: About 490 calories, 21g protein, 90g carbohydrate, 6g total fat (1g saturated), 4mg cholesterol, 885mg sodium.

Acorn Squash with White Beans & Sage

Preparation of this dish is fast and easy because the beans cook on the stovetop while the squash steams in the microwave.

PREP: 15 MINUTES   COOK: 20 MINUTES
MAKES 4 MAIN-DISH SERVINGS.

1 tablespoon olive oil
1 jumbo onion (1 pound), cut into
    1/4-inch pieces
1 medium carrot, peeled and cut into
    1/4-inch pieces
2 garlic cloves, crushed with
    garlic press
1 can (15 to 19 ounces) white
    kidney beans (cannellini),
    rinsed and drained
3/4 cup vegetable broth

1/4 teaspoon salt
1/4 teaspoon coarsely ground
    black pepper
3 teaspoons chopped fresh
    sage leaves
2 small acorn squashes (about
    12 ounces each)
1 medium tomato, coarsely chopped
grated Parmesan cheese (optional)

1. In nonstick 12-inch skillet, heat oil over medium-high heat until hot. Add onion, carrot, and garlic; cook, stirring occasionally, until vegetables are tender and golden, about 15 minutes. Add beans, broth, salt, pepper, and 2 teaspoons chopped sage; heat to boiling. Remove skillet from heat; cover and keep warm.

2. Meanwhile, cut each acorn squash lengthwise in half and remove seeds and strings. Place squash halves in 3-quart microwave-safe baking dish. Cover and cook in microwave oven on High until squash is fork-tender, 6 to 8 minutes.

3. Place squash halves, cut side up, on platter. Fill each half with one-fourth of bean mixture; sprinkle with chopped tomato and remaining 1 teaspoon chopped sage. Serve with Parmesan, if you like.

Each serving: About 250 calories, 9g protein, 47g carbohydrate, 5g total fat (1g saturated), 0mg cholesterol, 520mg sodium.

Tip

This recipe was tested in a 1,100-watt microwave oven. If your microwave has more or less power, it may be necessary to make adjustments in cooking times to reach desired degree of doneness.

Couscous with Garbanzo Beans

Couscous with Garbanzo Beans

A meatless entrée fragrant with the flavors of Morocco—warm spices, green olives, and garlic—gets a quick start from seasoned couscous mix.

PREP: 15 MINUTES COOK: 11 MINUTES
MAKES 4 MAIN-DISH SERVINGS.

1 box (5.6 ounces) couscous
  (Moroccan pasta) with toasted
  pine nuts
1/3 cup dark seedless raisins
1 tablespoon olive oil
1 medium zucchini, cut lengthwise
  in half, then crosswise into
  1/2-inch pieces
1 garlic clove, crushed with
  garlic press

3/4 teaspoon ground cumin
3/4 teaspoon ground coriander
1/8 teaspoon ground red pepper
  (cayenne)
2 cans (15 to 19 ounces each)
  garbanzo beans, rinsed and drained
1/2 cup chopped pimiento-stuffed
  olives (salad olives), drained
1/4 cup water

1. Prepare couscous as label directs, except add raisins to cooking water.
2. Meanwhile, in nonstick 12-inch skillet, heat oil over medium-high heat until hot. Add zucchini and cook, stirring occasionally, 5 minutes. Add garlic, cumin, coriander, and ground red pepper, and cook, stirring, 30 seconds. Add beans, olives, and water, and cook, stirring frequently, until heated through, 5 minutes.
3. Add the cooked couscous to bean mixture, and toss gently. Spoon into serving bowl.

Each serving: About 555 calories, 20g protein, 101g carbohydrate, 10g total fat (1g saturated), 0mg cholesterol, 1,110mg sodium.

Tofu in Spicy Brown Sauce

We used a package of frozen Asian-style vegetables to save chopping time. For best quality, buy *firm* tofu (bean curd), sold in sealed packages.

PREP: 15 MINUTES   COOK: 20 MINUTES
MAKES 6 MAIN-DISH SERVINGS.

2 packages (1 pound each) firm tofu, rinsed and drained
1 cup vegetable broth
$1/3$ cup reduced-sodium soy sauce
1 tablespoon brown sugar
1 tablespoon cornstarch
2 tablespoons seasoned rice vinegar
$1/8$ teaspoon crushed red pepper
$1/2$ cup cold water

1 package (16 ounces) frozen Asian-style mixed vegetables
1 tablespoon vegetable oil
3 garlic cloves, crushed with garlic press
2 tablespoons minced, peeled fresh ginger
3 green onions, trimmed and sliced
steamed white rice (optional)

1. Place 4 layers of paper towel in 15 1/2" by 10 1/2" jelly-roll pan. Cut each piece of tofu horizontally in half. Place tofu on towels in pan; top with 4 more layers of paper towel. Gently press tofu with hand to extract excess moisture. Let stand 1 minute; repeat once, using more paper towels.

2. Cut tofu into 1 1/2-inch cubes; set aside. In small bowl, with fork or wire whisk, mix broth, soy sauce, brown sugar, cornstarch, vinegar, crushed red pepper, and water until blended.

3. In nonstick 12-inch skillet, heat frozen vegetables, covered, over medium-high heat 5 minutes, stirring occasionally. Uncover and cook until liquid has evaporated, stirring occasionally, about 2 minutes longer. Transfer vegetables to bowl. Wipe skillet dry.

4. In same skillet, heat oil over medium heat until hot. Add garlic and ginger; cook 1 minute. Stir broth mixture; add to skillet and heat to boiling over medium-high heat; stirring. Boil 1 minute. Stir in vegetables and tofu; cook until heated through, about 5 minutes. Sprinkle with green onions before serving. Serve with steamed rice, if you like.

Each serving without rice: About 295 calories, 27g protein, 20g carbohydrate, 16g total fat (2g saturated), 0mg cholesterol, 870mg sodium.

Tofu in Spicy Brown Sauce

Thai Tofu Stir-Fry

Fresh ginger and basil are frequently used in Thai cooking. For the best flavor, do not substitute ground ginger or dried basil.

PREP: 30 MINUTES   COOK: 25 MINUTES
MAKES 4 MAIN-DISH SERVINGS.

1 package (16 ounces) firm tofu, drained and cut into 1-inch cubes
1 tablespoon curry powder
1 tablespoon grated, peeled fresh ginger
1 tablespoon soy sauce
1 tablespoon Asian fish sauce (nuoc nam, see Tip page 50)
6 teaspoons vegetable oil
1 medium head bok choy (about 1 pound), cut crosswise into 1-inch pieces

1 medium zucchini, cut into bite-size pieces
3 green onions, trimmed and cut into 2-inch pieces
8 ounces medium mushrooms, trimmed and cut into 1/4-inch-thick slices
1 medium red pepper, sliced
3/4 cup vegetable broth
1 1/2 teaspoons cornstarch
1/2 cup packed fresh basil leaves, chopped

1. In medium bowl, gently toss tofu cubes with curry powder, ginger, soy sauce, and fish sauce.

2. In nonstick 12-inch skillet, heat 2 teaspoons oil over medium-high heat. Add bok choy, zucchini, and green onions, and cook until vegetables are tender-crisp, about 8 minutes. Transfer vegetables to large bowl.

3. With slotted spoon, remove the tofu from the curry mixture; reserve curry mixture.

4. In same skillet, heat 2 teaspoons oil. Add tofu and cook until lightly browned, about 5 minutes, gently stirring occasionally. Transfer tofu to bowl with bok choy mixture.

5. In same skillet, heat remaining 2 teaspoons oil. Add mushrooms and red pepper; cook until pepper is tender-crisp, about 8 minutes.

6. Into curry mixture in bowl, stir broth and cornstarch; stir into skillet with mushroom mixture. Heat to boiling; boil until sauce thickens slightly, about 1 minute. Return bok choy mixture to skillet. Add basil; heat through.

Each serving: About 295 calories, 24g protein, 17g carbohydrate, 18g total fat (2g saturated), 2mg cholesterol, 745mg sodium.

Tofu with Broccoli & Shiitake Mushrooms

We call for a bag of broccoli flowerets to save cutting and trimming time. Choose extra-firm tofu; other types will fall apart during stir-frying. To serve, spoon the saucy mixture over quick-cooking brown rice.

PREP: 25 MINUTES   COOK: 15 MINUTES
MAKES 4 MAIN-DISH SERVINGS.

3 tablespoons soy sauce
1 tablespoon brown sugar
1 tablespoon cornstarch
1 cup cold water
2 teaspoons vegetable oil
3 garlic cloves, crushed with garlic press
1 tablespoon grated, peeled fresh ginger
1/8 to 1/4 teaspoon crushed red pepper

1 bag (12 ounces) broccoli flowerets, cut into uniform pieces if necessary
8 ounces shiitake mushrooms, stems removed and caps thinly sliced
1 medium red pepper, cut into 1-inch pieces
1 package (15 ounces) extra-firm tofu, patted dry and cut into 1-inch cubes
3 green onions, trimmed and thinly sliced

1. In small bowl, whisk soy sauce, brown sugar, cornstarch, and cold water; set aside.

2. In deep nonstick 12-inch skillet, heat oil over medium-high heat until hot. Add garlic, ginger, and crushed red pepper, and cook, stirring constantly (stir-frying), 30 seconds. Add broccoli, mushrooms, and red pepper, and cook, covered, 8 minutes, stirring occasionally.

3. Add tofu and green onions, and cook, uncovered, 2 minutes, stirring occasionally. Stir soy-sauce mixture, and add to skillet; heat to boiling. Boil, stirring, 1 minute.

Each serving: About 225 calories, 16g protein, 23g carbohydrate, 9g total fat (1g saturated), 0mg cholesterol, 775mg sodium.

Curried Vegetable Stew

Curried Vegetable Stew

A fast, fragrant skillet dish flavored with rich Indian spices, raisins, and tomatoes. Serve over rice or with pita bread and plain yogurt.

PREP: 30 MINUTES   COOK: 40 MINUTES
MAKES 5 MAIN-DISH SERVINGS.

1 tablespoon olive oil
1 medium onion, coarsely chopped
5 cups small cauliflower flowerets
 (about 1 small head cauliflower)
4 medium carrots, peeled and each
 cut lengthwise in half, then
 crosswise into 1/4-inch-thick slices
1 tablespoon minced, peeled fresh
 ginger
3 garlic cloves, crushed with
 garlic press
1 tablespoon curry powder

1 teaspoon ground cumin
3/4 teaspoon salt
1/8 to 1/4 teaspoon ground red pepper
 (cayenne)
2 cans (15 to 19 ounces each)
 garbanzo beans, rinsed and drained
1 can (14 1/2 ounces) diced tomatoes
1/4 cup golden raisins
1/2 cup water
1/2 cup loosely packed fresh cilantro
 leaves, chopped

1. In nonstick 12-inch skillet, heat oil over medium heat. Add onion and cook, stirring occasionally, 5 minutes. Increase heat to medium-high; add cauliflower and carrots; cook, stirring occasionally, until vegetables are lightly browned, about 10 minutes. Add ginger, garlic, curry powder, cumin, salt, and ground red pepper; cook, stirring, 1 minute.

2. Add garbanzo beans, tomatoes with their juice, raisins, and water; heat to boiling over high heat. Reduce heat to low; cover and simmer, until vegetables are tender and sauce thickens slightly, 15 to 20 minutes. Stir in cilantro.

Each serving: About 430 calories, 18g protein, 74g carbohydrate, 10g total fat (1g saturated), 0mg cholesterol, 1,430mg sodium.

Potato Dumplings with Cabbage & Apples

Pierogi, Polish-style comfort food, are usually filled with meat, seafood, cheese, potatoes, or mushrooms. They can be quite time-consuming to prepare from scratch, but fortunately, excellent frozen varieties are available. Serve with a tomato salad and warm rolls. Get them ready while the cabbage cooks.

PREP: 5 MINUTES   COOK: 25 MINUTES
MAKES 4 MAIN-DISH SERVINGS.

1 package (16 to 19 ounces) frozen potato-and-onion pierogi
1 tablespoon butter or margarine
1 small onion, thinly sliced
1 small head green cabbage (1 1/2 pounds), trimed, cored, and sliced
1/2 cup vegetable broth
1/2 teaspoon salt
2 medium McIntosh apples (about 12 ounces)
2 teaspoons cider vinegar
1 tablespoon chopped fresh dill

1. In large saucepot, cook pierogi as label directs.

2. Meanwhile, in nonstick 12-inch skillet, melt butter over medium-low heat. Add onion and cook, stirring occasionally, until onion is tender and lightly browned, about 7 minutes.

3. Increase heat to medium-high; add cabbage, broth, and salt, and cook until cabbage is tender, about 10 minutes. While cabbage is cooking, core and cut apples into 1/4-inch-thick wedges.

4. Add apples and vinegar to skillet with cabbage, and cook until apples soften, about 5 minutes.

5. Drain pierogi; toss with cabbage mixture and dill.

Each serving: About 355 calories, 9g protein, 64g carbohydrate, 7g total fat (3g saturated), 8mg cholesterol, 941mg sodium.

Potato Dumplings with Cabbage & Apples

Barley-Vegetable Stew

A simple Italian gremolata of parsley, garlic, and lemon tops the stew to add a distinctive tangy element.

PREP: 10 MINUTES   COOK: 15 MINUTES
MAKES 4 MAIN-DISH SERVINGS.

1 cup quick-cooking barley
1 tablespoon olive oil
1 package (20 ounces) peeled butternut squash, cut into 1/2-inch pieces (4 cups)
2 medium stalks celery, cut into 1/2-inch pieces
1 medium onion, chopped
1 jar (14 to 16 ounces) marinara sauce

1 package (9 ounces) frozen cut green beans
1 cup vegetable broth
1/2 teaspoon salt
1/4 teaspoon ground black pepper
1/2 cup loosely packed fresh parsley leaves, chopped
1/2 teaspoon grated fresh lemon peel
1 small garlic clove, minced

1. Cook barley as label directs.

2. Meanwhile, in nonstick 12-inch skillet, heat oil over medium-high heat. Add squash, celery, and onion; cover and cook, stirring occasionally, until lightly browned, about 10 minutes. Stir in marinara sauce, frozen beans, broth, salt, and pepper. Simmer, uncovered, until slightly thickened, about 4 minutes.

3. In small bowl, combine parsley, lemon peel, and garlic; set aside.

4. Drain liquid from barley, if any. Stir barley into vegetables. Sprinkle with parsley mixture to serve.

Each serving: About 320 calories, 9g protein, 60g carbohydrate, 7g total fat (1g saturated), 0mg cholesterol, 985mg sodium.

INDEX

PHOTO CREDITS

Page 2: Mark Thomas **Page 3:** Mark Pederson **Page 6:** Alan Richardson **Page 12:** Alan Richardson **Pages 14-15:** Brian Hagiwara **Page 21:** Ann Stratton **Page 24:** Mark Pederson **Page 29:** Mark Pederson **Page 31:** Mark Thomas **Page 32:** Mark Thomas **Page 35:** Mark Thomas **Page 41:** Mark Thomas **Page 42:** Ann Stratton **Page 45:** Alan Richardson **Page 46:** Brian Hagiwara **Page 51:** Brian Hagiwara **Page 56:** Brian Hagiwara **Page 59:** Brian Hagiwara **Pages 60-61:** Mark Thomas **Page 62:** Rita Maas **Page 65:** Alan Richardson **Page 67:** Mark Thomas **Page 68:** Mark Thomas **Page 71:** Alan Richardson **Page 72:** Brian Hagiwara **Page 75:** Mark Pederson **Page 78:** Brian Hagiwara **Page 83:** Rita Maas **Page 84:** Brian Hagiwara **Page 89:** Alan Richardson **Page 92:** Brian Hagiwara **Page 95:** Mark Pederson **Page 96:** Mark Thomas **Page 99:** Mark Thomas **Page 101:** Alan Richardson **Page 103:** Brian Hagiwara **Page 105:** Alan Richardson **Page 106:** Brian Hagiwara **Page 109:** Brian Hagiwara **Page 112:** Alan Richardson **Pages 116-117:** Brian Hagiwara **Page 120:** Brian Hagiwara **Page 123:** Brian Hagiwara **Page 124:** Brian Hagiwara **Page 129:** Alan Richardson **Page 130:** Peter Ardito **Page 133:** Alan Richardson **Page 137:** Rita Maas **Page 144:** Brian Hagiwara **Pages 146-147:** Alan Richardson **Page 149:** Martin Jacobs **Page 152:** Steven Mark Needham **Page 157:** Alan Richardson **Page 159:** Alan Richardson **Page 162:** Alan Richardson **Page 165:** Alan Richardson **Page 166:** Brian Hagiwara **Page 171:** Alan Richardson **Page 173:** Ann Stratton **Page 174-175:** Alan Richardson **Page 177:** Alan Richardson **Page 178:** Alan Richardson **Page 181:** Rita Maas **Page 182:** Alan Richardson **Page 185:** Alan Richardson **Page 190:** Brian Hagiwara **Page 196:** Rita Maas **Page 199:** Alan Richardson **Page 208:** Alan Richardson

METRIC EQUIVALENTS

The recipes that appear in this cookbook use the standard United States method for measuring liquid and dry or solid ingredients (teaspoons, tablespoons, and cups). The information on this chart is provided to help cooks outside the U.S. successfully use these recipes. All equivalents are approximate.

METRIC EQUIVALENTS FOR DIFFERENT TYPES OF INGREDIENTS

A standard cup measure of a dry or solid ingredient will vary in weight depending on the type of ingredient. A standard cup of liquid is the same volume for any type of liquid. Use the following chart when converting standard cup measures to grams (weight) or milliliters (volume).

Standard Cup	Fine Powder (e.g. flour)	Grain (e.g. rice)	Granular (e.g. sugar)	Liquid Solids (e.g. butter)	Liquid (e.g. milk)
1	140 g	150 g	190 g	200 g	240 ml
3/4	105 g	113 g	143 g	150 g	180 ml
2/3	93 g	100 g	125 g	133 g	160 ml
1/2	70 g	75 g	95 g	100 g	120 ml
1/3	47 g	50 g	63 g	67 g	80 ml
1/4	35 g	38 g	48 g	50 g	60 ml
1/8	18 g	19 g	24 g	25 g	30 ml

USEFUL EQUIVALENTS FOR LIQUID INGREDIENTS BY VOLUME

1/4 tsp	=						1 ml
1/2 tsp	=						2 ml
1 tsp	=						5 ml
3 tsp	=	1 tbls	=			1/2 fl oz =	15 ml
		2 tbls	=	1/8 cup	=	1 fl oz =	30 ml
		4 tbls	=	1/4 cup	=	2 fl oz =	60 ml
		5 1/3 tbls	=	1/3 cup	=	3 fl oz =	80 ml
		8 tbls	=	1/2 cup	=	4 fl oz =	120 ml
		10 2/3 tbls	=	2/3 cup	=	5 fl oz =	160 ml
		12 tbls	=	3/4 cup	=	6 fl oz =	180 ml
		16 tbls	=	1 cup	=	8 fl oz =	240 ml
		1 pt	=	2 cups	=	16 fl oz =	480 ml
		1 qt	=	4 cups	=	32 fl oz =	960 ml
						33 fl oz =	1000 ml = 1 l

USEFUL EQUIVALENTS FOR DRY INGREDIENTS BY WEIGHT
(To convert ounces to grams, multiply the number of ounces by 30.)

1 oz	=	1/16 lb	=	30 g
4 oz	=	1/4 lb	=	120 g
8 oz	=	1/2 lb	=	240 g
12 oz	=	3/4 lb	=	360 g
16 oz	=	1 lb	=	480 g

USEFUL EQUIVALENTS FOR LENGTH
(To convert inches to centimeters, multiply the number of inches by 2.5.)

1 in	=			2.5 cm
6 in	=	1/2 ft	=	15 cm
12 in	=	1 ft	=	30 cm
36 in	=	3 ft	= 1 yd =	90 cm
40 in	=			100 cm = 1 m

USEFUL EQUIVALENTS FOR COOKING/OVEN TEMPERATURES

	Fahrenheit	Celsius	Gas Mark
Freeze Water	32° F	0° C	
Room Temperature	68° F	20° C	
Boil Water	212° F	100° C	
Bake	325° F	160° C	3
	350° F	180° C	4
	375° F	190° C	5
	400° F	200° C	6
	425° F	220° C	7
	450° F	230° C	8
Broil			Grill